ECONOMIC CRISIS

A Christian Perspective

Also published by SCM Press

Enough is Enough
John V. Taylor

Perspectives on Strikes
Edited by Ronald H. Preston

Theology in an Industrial Society
Margaret Kane

JOHN F. SLEEMAN

Economic Crisis:
A Christian Perspective

SCM PRESS LTD

334 00367 9

First published 1976
by SCM Press Ltd
58 Bloomsbury Street, London WC1

Type set by Gloucester Typesetting Co. Ltd
and printed in Great Britain by
Fletcher & Son Ltd
Norwich

CONTENTS

PREFACE

This book arises out of the experience of trying to understand the working of the economy in the course of teaching and research in economics, while at the same time seeking to interpret it more deeply in the light of the Christian faith. Not many economists find it natural to think in theological terms, since the philosophical traditions of the subject tend to be humanist and utilitarian. Nor did many theologians have the grounding in economics which makes them feel at home in tackling practical issues about how we get our living.

It is hoped, therefore, that many will find helpful a book which tries to bring the two approaches together. It starts from the practical aspect of some of the inescapable economic issues in which we are all involved, such as inflation, wealth and poverty, the rich and poor worlds, growth and the environment, and how the industrial and commercial system is organized. These are treated in some detail, since it is felt that many readers will welcome a fair amount of description and analysis of these problems, with which they may not be familiar. The discussion of Christian social philosophy is a good deal more summary, since there has been plenty written on this already. What has not often been attempted before is to look at the practical economic issues in the light of the Christian philosophy, and see what we can draw from it in terms of lines of thought and action which Christians should be supporting.

The book is intended primarily for those who start from a Christian position, and hence it takes the basics of this very much for granted, without seeking to argue for them and justify them against alternative standpoints. It is hoped, however, that this has not been done in so dogmatic a way as to put off those who do not start from this position. Indeed, there must be many who would not call themselves Christians who yet share similar liberal, humane ideals and are equally concerned about the relevance of these to the strains and stresses of our present economic crisis. This book may perhaps be found useful by them also. Indeed, it may be a means of bridging any gaps in understanding between what one might call Christian humanists and non-Christian humanists, by providing a common meeting place of concern for the issues which so urgently confront us at present.

I

Introduction

1. *A world in crisis*

We are constantly being told, in the press, on radio and television and by public figures of every kind, that we are living in a time of crisis. Indeed, in many ways this is true. Prices are rising fast in most of the countries of the world, and the rate in much of Western Europe is now approaching the 20% annual level previously associated only with Latin America. Incomes are also rising, but wage and salary earners find it hard to keep pace with the cost of living, and those on fixed incomes have not a hope of doing so. Yet every rise in pay, if employers pass it on in higher prices, means another turn of the wage-price spiral. If they do not pass it on, it means that firms have not the cash to pay their bills and must lay off workers.

On a world scale the steep rise of foodstuff and raw material prices was the main factor in sparking off the inflationary explosion from 1973 onwards. Oil prices quadrupled and that not only put up energy costs throughout the world, but set up a grave imbalance in the world's payments system. Although the problem of recycling the oil producing countries' huge surpluses and expanding their limited import capacity proved less serious than feared, yet balance of payments deficits and rising costs put an end to the long period of growth of world trade and induced a general slump. There was a danger that this would be intensified by the efforts of the main industrial countries to cut down their imports through deflationary policies of dear money and restricted public spending and thus mutually cripple one another's exports. Meanwhile the poor countries of the Third World were even worse hit, since they had to pay much more out of their scarce earnings of foreign exchange to get the oil which was essential to their industries and transport.

The crisis is not only an economic one; it is political also. At home, thirty years of full employment and rising real incomes have led to rising aspirations and impatience at still persisting inequalities and insecurities. If factories close down, for instance, workers are no longer prepared to accept this philosophically as an inevitable misfortune like the weather. They demand the right to work and are often prepared to occupy the plant in protest. If they see others getting pay increases which they feel leave them behind, they are more prepared to take industrial action. Recently we have seen strikes by teachers, nurses, radiographers, power station engineers and other groups for whom such conduct would have been almost unthinkable not so long ago. Stoppages in the public services have become commonplace in Britain, as indeed they have been for longer in France and Italy, and they have played their part in inducing a greater sense of unease and insecurity. If laws are passed which considerable groups of people feel to be unjust, there is greater willingness to refuse to obey them, as the examples of the Industrial Relations Act and the Housing Finance Act have shown.

Widespread fears are expressed that the country may be becoming ungovernable, and these are reflected in indecisive election results giving no party an adequate majority. The electors appear to want a government able to deal with the country's problems, but to be unwilling to accept the kind of measures which governments put forward in order to do so. Clashes between the police and groups of pickets during strikes and groups of protestors during demonstrations further arouse fears of a breakdown of law and order, and this is heightened by the tragic and apparently unending violence in Northern Ireland, with its spillover into England through the IRA's bomb activities. Retired military men begin to talk about forming citizens' volunteer forces in order to assist the civil authorities in the event of a breakdown.

Political strains and stresses in Britain are relatively slight compared with those in many other countries, although our economic difficulties seem to be greater. We have not experienced the bitterness and the violence of the American cities and campuses in the later sixties, nor a traumatic experience like that of France in 1968, nor the endemic unrest of present-day Italy. That there should be such a feeling of insecurity and uncertainty is largely because of the contrast with the certainty and security which we have known for so long. Such things might happen in other countries, we used to say, but they could never happen here.

What is happening world-wide is really a crisis of rising aspirations among the poor and underprivileged wherever they are found. It may be those in the West who feel that they have not got the pay or the security which others enjoy and which they feel is their due because of the importance of the work that they do. Or it may be those in the under-developed countries revolting against their age-old poverty and the domination of the world by the rich countries. People are increasingly unwilling to accept the ethos of 'the rich man in his castle, the poor man at his gate, God made them, high or lowly, and ordered their estate.'

2. *What is God saying? Why is there no clear proclamation?*

As Christians we believe that God is speaking to us out of this situation. We believe that this is his world, that he is active in it, and that his word can be heard in the events of human history. We believe that it is the church's duty to proclaim what God is doing and what he would have us do. We believe that his purposes are to be seen among the aspirations and hopes and fears of men, whether they themselves are conscious of it or not. So Amos of old denounced the selfish indifference of the rich and the unjust suffering of the poor in Israel in the eighth century before Christ. So Jeremiah a century and a half later proclaimed that the inevitable judgment of a just God on his faithless people was to be seen in the fall of Jerusalem before Nebuchadnezzar of Babylon. So in the Middle Ages the theologians denounced usury and insisted on the just price and the just wage. So in later times Wilberforce campaigned against the slave trade and Shaftesbury against exploitation in the factories, and Methodism led working men to organize themselves into trade unions and the early branches of the Labour Party, in order to assert their dignity and assure a reasonable living.

We cannot doubt that God is at work in the turmoil of our world today, in inflation, in industrial unrest and political uncertainty, in the aspirations of the Third World. He is calling on us to recognize him and join him in his work. He has a word for us to proclaim to our contemporaries, a word of judgment, of challenge, of hope, of comfort in the true sense of strength in times of doubt and fear. Yet the voice of the church, and of Christians generally, seems strangely silent. True, the Good News of personal salvation in Christ is still being faithfully proclaimed. Many are hearing it and finding it still brings abundant life. But others are unable to hear because it seems to be proclaimed in a too purely personal way, to involve a kind of escape from the real and immediate economic and political problems which surround them. Surely God must have something to say about these things too. Men and women are puzzled. If we face such a severe crisis, why is there no clear guidance? Our leaders, political, intellectual and spiritual, seem to be divided and uncertain themselves.

Why, then, is there no clear proclamation today? It seems to me that there are at least three strong reasons. First, there is no accepted body of standards and principles to which to appeal. Second, there is a great reluctance to meet complex economic and political situations with mere moral platitudes. Third, our traditional church leaders do not themselves have the training and experience which would make them at home in these fields.

First, unlike the position in Israel of old, or even in Europe up to, say, the nineteenth century, there is a lack of an accepted body of principles and beliefs to which to appeal. Although there were many backsliders in Israel in the days of Amos and in Judah in the days of Jeremiah, who disregarded the law of Yahweh and even followed strange gods, yet the people as a whole accepted that they were in a covenant relationship with their God and that this involved an obligation to keep his laws. Similarly, in the Europe of the Middle Ages, and generally up to the nineteenth century, the Christian ethic and world-view were accepted as the norm. This was true even though it seems to us that their expression in social terms often reflected too much the values of a static society in which everyone had his accepted place with its duties.

Nowadays this is no longer so. For the majority, the Christian world-view has lost acceptability and even the Christian ethic is widely criticized, especially since it is felt that its practical applications are too much concerned with defending the *status quo*. Therefore an appeal in terms of 'Thus saith the Lord' and calling for the acceptance of traditional laws based on the Ten Commandments is liable to fall on deaf ears.

Among Christians also there is an unwillingness to accept authoritarian guidance of this sort. Rightly, Christian men and women feel that they have come of age intellectually and morally. They must work out for themselves the meaning of obedience in a society much more complex and fast changing than that of their ancestors. They are not going to do what they are told by ecclesiastical authorities when it comes to questions about their way of life, or the position of their professional group, or the political party which they should follow, or even on more traditional issues of Christian morals such as contraception and abortion.

Second, there is a great reluctance on the part of those in positions of leadership in the church to respond to the complexities of the modern political and economic situation by stating moral platitudes. They are well aware that there are no clear-cut black and white solutions to most of these problems. You cannot say, for instance, that inflation is all due to the greed and irresponsibility of trade unions, or the greed and incompetence of business men, or the incompetence and lust for power of politicians. You cannot blame the present world economic crisis simply on the opportunism of the Arab oil producers, without going into all the complexities of the Arab-Israeli dispute. You cannot simply blame the shortsightedness of political leaders without looking at the problems of leadership in the United States in the aftermath of Watergate and the Vietnam War, or the German in-built fears of inflation, or the insecurities of the Russian leadership in the face of the aspirations of their people and the challenge of China – and many other things besides.

There is hardly a problem or conflict in the world in which all the contending parties do not have a strong and well arguable case, and on which experts will not differ widely in their analysis of the rights and wrongs. Small wonder, then, that church leaders hesitate to confront such situations with statements such as the need to love one's neighbour, or do a fair day's work, or respect law and order and properly constituted authority. Profound though most of these are in their implications, especially the first of them, yet these implications nevertheless need to be worked out by those involved in each situation, in the light of their own experience. If they are merely stated as being what God is saying, true though this may be, they are bound to sound platitudinous. This is the more true if they are propounded by church leaders who by reason of their office are rarely themselves directly involved in such situations.

This brings us to the third point. Church leaders traditionally have rarely had the type of training or experience which makes it easy for them to give the kind of lead on economic and political questions which they might wish to give. By and large, the initial academic training of bishops, moderators, Presidents of Conference, divinity professors and similar dignitaries has tended to be in the classics, or history, or philosophy and similar disciplines, and rarely in psychology, economics, political science or sociology. This is not to make undue claims for the social sciences as mental disciplines as against the older humanities, but with all their limitations they do direct the attention of those who follow them to the subject matter of modern social controversy. Such an initial grounding has naturally been followed by a training in theology which, in recent decades, has itself tended to suffer from the fragmentation of academic life and has become unduly detached from other disciplines, the more so if pursued in the rarefied atmosphere of a theological college.

Few of them have had any great personal experience of the worlds of industry, business, politics or the public service before embarking on the full-time ministry. Many of them have nevertheless achieved a remarkable width of sympathy and concern for the problems faced by men immersed in the rough and tumble of daily life. All the same, their own professional life has inevitably been largely taken up with the often in-bred minutiae of church organization.

Most church leaders are well aware of this, and naturally feel inhibited against making pronouncements about fields in which they do not feel themselves to be at home. Moreover, this lack of common experience means that unfortunately there has been all too little cross-fertilization of thought between theology and the social sciences such as political science or economics. There has thus never been developed an adequate body of thinking and experience out of which meaningful guidance could be given.

3. *Whose responsibility is it? Who is the church?*

But are we looking in the right place if we expect church leaders to make pronouncements? After all, who is the church? Is it not all of us who claim to be members of it, whatever our calling and experience? St Paul reminds us that the one body has many members and that these have different functions. There are prophets, teachers, pastors, healers, administrators and so on, but all of them are to use their gifts for the building up of the body (I. Cor. 12). We have tended to forget this far too much and to expect all the leadership in every field to come from the full time ministers of the word and sacraments. These have their own most vital contribution to make, but the lay members, each with their own experience arising out of their calling in life, should be making an active contribution also to the thinking and witness of the church, and not expect merely to pay their dues and be instructed.

Thus if 'the church' is to give a lead in proclaiming God's word about economic and political questions, it will be those engaged in economics and politics, whether as practitioners or as students and teachers, who will have to accept the responsibility. And here the academic professionals have one advantage over the practitioners, in being free to sit back and survey the scene from a little distance, and thus perhaps get a clearer and rather less biased view, though always with the danger of too much abstraction. If they can manage to set alongside their professional expertise the theological insight which can come from membership of the Christian fellowship, so that each illuminates, judges and interpenetrates the other, then perhaps they will have something worthwhile to say.

That is what this book is trying to do, humbly and hesitantly, but in the belief that there is a real need for such an attempt to explain what God is saying to us in the situation in which he has placed us at the present time.

4. *Plan of the argument*

Since I am an economist, the book concentrates on the economic aspects of present-day problems, though it soon becomes clear that these cannot be separated from the political and social aspects. The bulk of the work therefore consists of studies of some of the main economic issues of our day, in an attempt to bring out the essential factors involved in them, and the moral and philosophical questions to which they give rise. In each case an attempt is made to look at them in the light of the understanding of the world which is derived from the Christian faith.

Before this can be done profitably, however, it is necessary to look more closely at the general question of whether there can be a Christian economic and social philosophy, as distinct from the holding of different philosophies by Christians. This is the subject matter of chapter 2.

Chapters 3 to 7 then take up in succession the main economic issues. Inflation comes first, because it is the predominant immediate issue and because of its drastic effects on the whole life of the community. Then the question of fair shares within the nation is dealt with, why there is still poverty and lack of opportunity and what effects they have on the common life. This leads on to a consideration of fair shares internationally, the division of the world between rich and poor countries, and its implications. The consideration of how we use available means naturally leads us to consider growth and environment, and whether continued economic growth is possible in view of the strain on resources and the effects of pollution. Out of all these arises a study of economic organization and participation, what are the effects of different ways of organizing and controlling the economic system and how can these be modified to enable us to use material and human resources more responsibly for the good of all.

In the final chapter an attempt is made to draw out of the discussion certain more specific conclusions about how an effective Christian approach to the economic order might be developed. On the basis of these a personal view is given of some of the ways in which one would hope to see the actual economic system growing and changing so as to come nearer to being what its Creator intended it to be.

In all these chapters a considerable amount of space has inevitably to be given to description and analysis. Before we can say anything effective about Christian responsibility in these fields, we must first understand the facts of the situation, analyse them in terms of their deeper underlying causes and consequences, and discuss the various policy measures which have been attempted or advocated to deal with them. Indeed, this is part of our responsibility, and it is particularly the responsibility of those who have expertise and experience in the economic and political fields to use them to help those whose experience is different. Only so can we hope to arrive at a fuller and more informed understanding.

It is only after this has been done that we can bring to bear on the situation the particular interpretations and insights which arise out of Christian beliefs about the nature of man and the universe. Hence in each of chapters 3 to 7 the description and analysis are followed by a final section in which the attempt is made to explore how far these insights can throw new light on an often tangled situation, and what lines of action by Christians they may suggest.

2

Can there be a Christian Economic or Political Philosophy?

1. *What does Christianity imply?*

Acceptance of Christianity essentially implies devotion to a person. First and foremost, Christians are those who have encountered and been influenced by the historical personage, Jesus of Nazareth, and come to see in him the one in whom God has manifested himself to the world.[1] In him they have seen the love of God overcoming human weakness and selfishness by allowing men to do their worst, to misunderstand him, reject him and put him to death. In him they have seen the truth of God overcoming human falsities by the word which he spoke and lived. In him they have seen the power of God shown in apparent weakness, accepting what human power could do and overcoming it by this acceptance. In his resurrection they believe that the love, the truth and the power of God are vindicated as victorious. So they have come to accept that in the puzzling and uncertain world, he is the one who has the words of everlasting life, the one who can give meaning and purpose and strength. As he claimed to be, they find that he is indeed the way, the truth and the life.

But Christianity means not only acceptance of a person and devotion to him; it also means membership of a community. Men and women are not meant to be solitary. They need companionship and fellowship if they are to develop and be fully persons. What God means human life to be like cannot be shown forth fully in individual lives; it must be embodied in the life of a community. The church is intended to be the fellowship in which its members can grow to fullness of life by their mutual interaction one on another. In it the world should be able to see the pattern of a truly living, loving, sharing, serving community, a model in fact of what all human community should be.

The church has grievously failed to show this forth. In its days of success it has often been guilty of triumphalism, seeking earthly power and pomp, forgetful of its call to be a servant. Throughout most of its history it has been rent by schisms, and each fragment has often appeared to give more of its energies to anathematizing or persecuting its opponents than to showing forth the love of God. Too often it has been inward looking, wrapped up in its own concerns, the details of worship, the maintenance of its organization. Yet the essence of the divine community is still present, wherever church members are faithful to their founder and to his command to love and serve, and to the prompting of the Spirit, who according to his promise guides and pervades his church.

Yet Christianity does not merely mean devotion to a person and membership of a community. Like other religions, such as Islam or Buddhism, and like secular social philosophies such as Marxism or scientific humanism, it involves acceptance of a world view. There is a distinctive Christian view of the world, less clear-cut perhaps than that of Marxism, but characteristic nevertheless. It implies, for instance, that all men have the capacity to know and respond to God's love and truth, even though they may be prevented by their heredity and environment from actually realizing this and accepting them. It therefore implies that all men are of equal value to God, though they are of very different temperaments and capacities. They must therefore be treated as such by their fellows, and this means that they must be accepted as persons and not used as instruments of other people's purposes. It implies that the true and worthwhile way of life is that of self-giving, in love to others and in service of them, and not that of self-seeking. It implies that, whatever appearances may be to the contrary, love is stronger than hate, truth than falsehood, trust than fear.

The Christian view recognizes nevertheless that men are weak and constantly fail in their endeavours to achieve justice and righteousness. As St Paul puts it, there are two contending forces in human nature. There is the higher nature which loves what is good and strives for it, and the lower nature which constantly frustrates this desire and gives way to what is selfish and evil (Rom. 7.19–24). Hence a perfect society cannot be hoped for in this world, and men's best endeavours will always be marred by self-seeking.[2] Yet this is not a cause for despair, but rather for willingness to accept one's own weakness and need of forgiveness and to extend compassion and forgiveness to others. For the Christian believes that in the strength of Christ's victory it is possible to rise again from defeat and continue to strive for justice and love.

Thus the world-view of Christianity is one which arises out of commitment to a person and experience of following him in the fellowship of the community, rather than out of abstract metaphysical speculation. The meaning of this experience has to be thought out and expressed in a clear and articulate way, in terms of principles for Christian living and Christian understanding of the nature of the world and of human society. But these principles and the theories based on them must always be tested in the light of experience and held under judgment by it. Christian theology and philosophy are a guide to Christian living, not a substitute for it.

Any attempt to work out a Christian economic and political philosophy must be undertaken on this basis. We proceed, therefore, to draw out of the Christian experience certain general principles which can guide our understanding of the world in which men have to get their living and live together in society.

2. *What principles are implied by this for our approach to economic and political problems?*

(*a*) *The imperative of love means the willing of justice with generosity*

First, the overriding imperative of Christian action is that of love, and this must apply not only in personal relations, but also in the exercise of political and economic responsibility. We are called upon to love our neighbour as ourself and that means willing what is best for him and striving to achieve it. Our neighbour is everyone with whom we come into contact, or whom our actions can affect. To the unfortunate traveller on the road to Jericho it was the alien Samaritan who proved to be the neighbour, for he did what was needed in the situation.

Our lives and our actions affect those of our neighbours at all sorts of levels in addition to our direct relationships with our families and friends and those who live near us. By the way in which we do our jobs we affect our colleagues, our bosses and customers or clients, and the general public who depend upon our organization for efficient service. This applies whether we work in a factory, shop or office, or as a teacher, doctor, nurse, administrator, or whatever. By the way we spend our money, or save it and invest it, we have an even wider influence. Through the market we set other people to work, or condemn them to redundancy, we cause raw materials and components to be ordered, imports to be brought from the ends of the earth. If we deposit our money in the bank, or lend it to a building society, or buy shares in a company, our actions have equally widespread repercussions.

Our political influence is widespread also. We affect the nature and policy of our government, national and local, by the way in which we cast our vote. We exercise influence also by the party which we support, the causes which engage our interest, the organizations which we join. By the way in which we react to the news in press, radio and television, and the way in which we discuss it with our friends, we play a vital part in creating and influencing public opinion. Some of us, through our trade union or professional association, or through voluntary societies, can play a more active part as members of pressure groups bringing a direct impact to bear on the government.

In all these spheres of indirect influence the imperative of love finds expression in the willing of justice with generosity. It means working as far as possible to ensure that each individual or group gets a fair share of the world's goods, a fair opportunity to use his or her talents and gifts for the benefit of all, a fair chance to become a full person. It means that care must be taken that the strong do not dispossess or oppress the weak.

Having said this is merely to state the complexity of the problem, for in most economic and political situations there is an inevitable conflict of interests. Justice for one group must be balanced off against justice for another. The wage or salary earner wants higher pay and a better standard of living, but the business firm must make profits if it is to pay for necessary materials and extend and improve its plant and be able to go on providing employment and selling a service. In politics, the government has to balance the spending of more money on education or health services or social security against the need to spend on defence or on aid to industry. It also has to consider the effects of the taxation needed to pay for its expenditure. How far should it come from income tax, or corporation tax, or value added tax, and what will be the effects of each of these on incentives to work or undertake business enterprises, or on the living standards of the less well off?

Thus a judgment has to be made as to what constitutes justice in any particular case, and Christians do not have any particular expertise in arriving at the most appropriate solution. The imperative of love may, however, perhaps suggest another principle, that of generosity, as a guide in the exercise of the inevitable choice. While love must always be concerned with justice, and with making sure that in meeting the needs of one group, those of another group are not overlooked or overridden, yet generosity would suggest that if the balance has to be weighed, it should be weighed in favour of those who are less well off and less able to take care of themselves. Thus it would be contrary to the spirit of generosity to be niggardly in caring for the needs of widows and old people and children from deprived homes, owing to an over-meticulous care for justice to the well off and powerful, and for the influential leaders of business, who are usually quite capable of making their interests known.

In particular, the concept of generosity should make members of any group wary of giving too much weight to justice for the interests of themselves and those like them, and aware of the danger of disguising self-centred concern as a concern for social justice. This is a principle which Christians in the comfortable middle classes in the rich industrial countries would do well to keep in mind, as they consider those less welloff in their own countries, and the mass of the poor and needy in the Third World.

(*b*) *A transcending of the world's standards, but an acceptance of the world as being the sphere of God's purposes*

The imperative of love, and its expression in terms of justice interpreted with generosity implies that a Christian economic and political philosophy must transcend the world's standards of what constitutes success, or happiness, or fulfilment. Yet at the same time it must be firmly anchored in the world as it is, with all its limitations, and not take off into Utopian fantasies. For the world, as it is, is the sphere of God's love and his purposes.

A Christian philosophy cannot accept as a desirable norm a situation in which men make it the chief aim in their lives to get more money, or power, or comfort, or influence for themselves, however much they may justify this by claiming that they do no harm to others who are free to do likewise. For Christians must maintain that such an aim is bound to lead to lack of concern for the interests of others, especially those who are weaker or less fortunate, and hence to grave social and political injustice. The rich tend to get richer and the powerful more powerful, while the poor and the weak are kept in poverty and weakness.[3] It will lead inevitably to mistrust and hatred and suspicion and a breakdown of understanding and community. Such a system can only be maintained by force and will be likely to break down ultimately in revolution, in the absence of counteracting forces to bring about greater social justice. It does violence to the personalities both of those who are losers, who become warped and bitter and frustrated and apathetic, and to the gainers, who become avaricious and fearful and uncharitable. It is not for nothing that Christ condemned the pursuit of riches, as much for its effect on the rich as for that on the poor.[4]

Yet the Christian must not take flight into an imaginary Utopian world in which everyone is generous and wise and loving. For this actual world is the world which God so loved that he gave his only begotten Son that all should believe in him and have eternal live (John 3.16). The Christian must be concerned with the establishment of a just and generous society in this world, and that means a willingness to recognize what is possible. The call to follow Christ on his road of generous self-giving must be proclaimed to all as the only truly worthwhile life, but we must recognize that all men are fallible. They will see and accept this ideal in different degrees. Some will only glimpse it dimly in terms, say, of an obligation to help those less fortunate. Others will seize on one aspect of it, say the call to generous personal giving of time and energy to the service of those in need. Others will seize on other aspects, such as a concern to work for a juster order by political means. None will arrive at it completely.

Christian social philosophy must therefore be directed towards achieving the justest and fairest and most equitable and workable economic and political system which it is practicable to envisage being built in a particular situation. We must start with men as they are, capable of generosity if their imagination is stirred, capable also of much selfishness, most of them with pressing immediate responsibilities and obligations. We must start with institutions as they are, the business firms we have, the trade unions, political parties, government departments and so on, with their workers, managers and shareholders, officials and rank and file members, civil servants and professional staff.

We must also start with the economic and political problems as they are, and the inescapable constraints which they impose. The economic problem turns on how to use natural and human resources in the most effective way to satisfy human wants. Hence it involves both the establishment of criteria by which we can judge whether resources are being used efficiently, and the introduction of incentives to persuade men and women to use their skills and talents in ways which enable these criteria to be satisfied. Thus what makes men give of their best is an essential part of the economic problem, but so also is the fact that at any given time or place resources are limited relative to the uses which could be made of them. If we use skills or materials or plant for one purpose, we cannot use them for another. Any programme for a better economic order must deal realistically with these issues.

The political problem turns on the use of power, on who is to decide what is to be done in the collective activity of society, how those who so decide are to persuade the population to co-operate in what they want done, and how the exercise of this power can be made responsible to those on whose behalf it is exercised. These, too, are inescapable facts of which any realistic political programme must take account.

(*c*) *A recognition of our own involvement in the world and in a particular society*

This two-fold recognition, that the Christian vision transcends the limitations of particular human societies and that it must at the same time be firmly earthed in them, applies also to the work and witness of individual Christians.

Christians must never be content merely to accept the standards and values of the social group which forms their background. Whether it is the ethos of the business man, the professional man or the shop-floor worker, that of the comfortable middle-class suburb or the working-class housing estate, that of conventional conservatism or of conventional socialism, that of Britain or the United States, of India or Nigeria, the Christian must strive always to hold it under the judgment of the love imperative of Christ. This is difficult to do, for we get used to accepting our conventional ways of thinking as being normal. It is also uncomfortable, for it challenges our accustomed securities, but we must not shrink from it.

At the same time we must be realistic in recognizing that we will never succeed in doing this completely. The accustomed ways of thought and standards of value in which we have grown up go very deep, so that we are apt to take as axioms of divine truth what are often largely prejudices based on unconsidered tradition. Thus middle-class professional people are apt to regard the less well-off and less secure manual workers as feckless, extravagant, afraid of steady work, always apt to strike, and so on. They in turn tend to regard the middle classes as snooty, self-centred, arrogant and grasping. Similar stereotypes affect the attitude of most people in the West to the inhabitants of the Third World, who still tend to be thought of as 'natives', living 'out there' in picturesque and primitive squalor.

In particular, since the church in the West is so largely middle class, there is a strong tendency for middle-class, professional prejudices to become rationalized into being accepted as Christian attitudes, without sufficient realization of the extent to which they are culturally based.

Christians must therefore recognize the extent to which their own beliefs and standards are likely to be biased, and be prepared to make allowances for it. Perhaps the best way to do this is to cultivate contacts with people of different backgrounds and beliefs. To enter into dialogue with others and try to understand their views with imaginative sympathy is at the same time to apply an essential critique to one's own views.

Nevertheless, this recognition of the likely bias of one's views is not a call to escape from one's background into a Utopian neutrality. We have to accept that we are what background and circumstances have made us, and do our best with it, and also to recognize that other people are what they have been made, and accept them and work with them in a common search for greater understanding.

For some the call may come to give up their present way of life and go off into some new and more radical way to which they feel God is calling them. Thus some feel they must join communes and other forms of alternative society, or others find that the call comes to serve overseas in a developing country. For most, however, the call is likely to be to continue in the work for which they are trained and among the colleagues and friends with whom they associate, but with the realization that this is not the whole world, and a vision of a wider truth by which it must always be judged.

Above all, there is a call to continued and hopeful involvement. We are often tempted to escape from the complications of society into a private world, of home, family and friends, of our job and promotion prospects, of sport, or art, or music, or whatever, or even into a purely personal religious piety. This temptation must be resisted for, with all our limitations, our place is in the world, not shirking its problems, but doing what we can towards finding a practical solution to those aspects of them that lie at hand. At the same time we need not worry if our efforts seem small and feeble, so long as we are doing what we can as well as we can. We believe that we are not alone and that whatever is done for God is not wasted.

3. *Can there be a Christian economic and social philosophy?*

In the light of all that we have seen so far, can there be such a thing as a Christian economic, political and social philosophy? Can we expect that Christians will come together to share a specifically Christian view of how society works and a specifically Christian programme of how it should develop? Or are any such expectations Utopian, and must we look rather to seeing Christians accepting a number of different so-called secular philosophies and embracing a variety of 'secular' programmes? The argument has to be developed further through a number of successive stages.

(*a*) *Christians will differ in their beliefs about the world*

First, we must accept, what we find in practice, that Christians will differ as widely as persons of other beliefs about the detailed ways in which they view the world and the specific values and aims which they find important. As we have already seen, this reflects differences in background and experience. Persons in managerial positions are likely, because of their experience and preoccupations, to view the problems of industry and the economic order in a different way from those working on the shop floor. More generally, those who have grown up with a middle-class background will tend to differ in the way in which they approach economic and political problems from those with a working-class background; though the existence of middle-class Labour supporters and working-class Tories make it clear that many people react against the accepted opinions of their group and adopt an opposite viewpoint.

The differences also arise from the differences of temperament, which themselves presumably reflect an intermingling of the influence of heredity and environment. It would seem that some people come by nature and experience to have a conservative outlook, tending to value continuity with the past, aware of the faults of the present set-up, but more afraid of the dangers of radical change. Others come to have a radical outlook, more acutely aware of the evils and shortcomings of the existing order and more eager to see it changed, even if it means running the risk of setting uncontrollable changes of trend in motion, and perhaps destroying much that is good.

This basic conservative-radical dichotomy resolves itself in practice into a continuum of outlooks from right to left along which most people are probably to be found. This is certainly true also of Christians. There is a strong Christian conservative tradition, concerned to preserve the traditional values, and inclined to view society as a kind of living organism, in which each group has its duties and its privileges, or as a family in which the senior members owe a duty to the junior members and vice versa. There is also a strong Christian radical tradition, which sees the gospel as a challenge to overthrow entrenched injustices and to bring new opportunities to the oppressed and needy, and which envisages the ideal Christian community more in socialist than in hierarchical terms.

A third factor which makes for difference of opinion and belief is the sheer complexity of the economic and political situation. No one can have a full understanding of every aspect of it, and each of us is influenced by the parts which we know best. Few of the choices to be made are straightforward ones between black and white, but they are nearly always between different shades of grey. If you want to follow one line of policy which will help one group of people, that will usually mean that you cannot follow another line which will help another. For instance, higher taxation on the better off and on companies may be necessary to improve education or pensions, but it may also mean that industry is short of capital for investment. Comprehensive schools may be the best means of giving equal educational opportunities to those with less favourable home backgrounds but, it is argued, they may also mean that the brightest children get less specialized attention. If we try to stop inflation by curbing government spending this may result in unemployment. Not unnaturally, there will be differences of opinion both as to the likeliest alternatives among possible outcomes of different choices of action, and as to the relative desirability of these outcomes.

(*b*) *Christians are under an obligation to hold their views under judgment*

Whatever their strongly-held beliefs about the nature of society and the way in which it should be organized, Christians are under an obligation to hold their views under the judgment of the faith which they profess. In the presence of Christ, the conservative authoritarianism of the Sadducee priests, the passionate legalism of the Pharisees and the violent nationalism of the Zealots were alike held under judgment, and their weaknesses were shown up as well as their strengths. So it must be with all our economic and political philosophies. There can be no room for the complacent conservatism which is content to accept the *status quo* because it is comfortable, and to sweep under the carpet all the injustices which it may conceal. There can be no place either for the heady and heedless radicalism that pushes on to its ideals, no matter what the injustice which it causes through the use of revolutionary violence or party authoritarianism. Christians in Latin America today find themselves in radical opposition to the often corrupt authoritarianism of their governing regimes. Archbishop Camara of Reçife in Brazil is only one distinguished example of this. Christians in the Communist countries, though with more difficulty, find themselves in, often silent but none of the less effective, opposition to the injustices and denials of freedom which arises from the one-party State.

Christians must also be alert to question their own deeply-held beliefs about the nature of society and in what ways it should develop. They must try to recognize when these are in fact rationalization of their own interests or those of their social group, rather than well-thought out convictions based on principle. In this they can learn from the Marxists, who were the first to teach us that political and social groups can be expected to have a large element of such rationalization in their thinking.

But when all allowances have been made for this, there will remain genuine differences of opinion, between Christians as between non-Christians, on important economic, social and political issues. And we should not be surprised at this. God's world is vast and his truth is great, and none of us can grasp more than a small part of them. But we can have the charity to accept that others will disagree with us and to respect their integrity and try to understand their reasons.

(*c*) *Are there any recognizable characteristics of Christian economic, social and political thinking?*

Christians, then, will find themselves in agreement with non-Christians of many different beliefs on most of the important issues of the day, and in disagreement with other Christians. Nevertheless, there are certain characteristics, arising out of basic Christian convictions, which one may expect to permeate the approach of all Christians to these issues. They should include the following:

1. Respect for other people, for their integrity, their interests, their right to a full life and the expression of their opinions. Christians should never be content to treat men and women merely as 'hands' to work in factories, or 'consumer units' to buy goods in shops, or as 'cases' to be processed by the social services. Although for many analytical purposes, especially where statistics are being used, classes of people must be aggregated in this sort of way, yet we must never forget that all men are brothers and sisters, made in God's image and loved by him just as we are. They cannot be used merely as means to an end, such as greater productivity, or greater strength for a political party, or greater influence in world politics. And this applies just as much to those pig-headed so and sos who disagree with us and can never understand the logic of our

arguments and the purity of our motives. They demand our respect as persons also.

2. Along with this should go a will for justice and for goodness. Christians will differ greatly about what this means in practice. Some will be prepared to accept authoritarian, though paternalistic, regimes as an alternative to the anarchy and disorder which might accompany attempts to secure greater freedom. Others will go all out for freedom and will hate authoritarianism, even though the cost may be anarchy and the breakdown of established order. Yet we should not expect to see Christians condoning, let alone actively supporting, regimes which are deliberately corrupt, inefficient and tyrannical, though we must of course recognize how difficult it is for those who have to live under such regimes to do anything effective to counteract them. Nor, on the other hand, should we expect to see them deliberately advocating violence or disorder for their own sakes, rather than as a reluctantly accepted price for trying to achieve a juster order.

3. There should also be a willingness to try to transcend one's own personal, class and group interests, together with a recognition that one is unlikely to be able to do so completely. Although we may have good reasons for believing that certain policies, say help for industrial investment, or increased educational opportunities for bright children, are of genuine benefit to the community as a whole, we must be prepared to recognize that our advocacy of them may in part be because they will help our firm to make profits, or our children to get to a better school. And if we come to believe that some other policy which cuts across our personal interests will genuinely be the best for the community, we must be prepared to advocate it also. Thus we may find ourselves driven to support the building of the new council estate near our select residence, or the tariff-free import of cheap cotton goods from India even though they hit profits and employment in our industry.

4. Along with this we may expect to see a willingness to accept that we have been mistaken. Christians should know that they are fallible, and when they make mistakes pride should not prevent them from admitting it and making amends in whatever way is called for. This may mean coming round to advocating policies which we have previously fiercely attacked, as well as making good any wrong which we have done to others.

5. Finally, Christians will be serious in their support of policies and opinions. There is no room in the Christian life for the cynical playing with ideas or causes just as a clever intellectual game or a titillating

sensation. The issues involved – people's livelihoods and welfare, war and peace, social justice – are too important for that. Those who never commit themselves never experience the fullness of worthwhile living.

But seriousness and commitment need not mean constant solemnity or lack of humour. Rather, a deep commitment and a deep seriousness, because they are rooted not in our feeble efforts but in God's purposes and power, can bring a freedom and a joyous gaiety which can permeate the most strenuous endeavour. The really committed men and women are in our experience usually the richest in human sympathy and human understanding of the follies and ridiculousness of life.

So Christians, though serious, should not be pompous or self-righteous. If we know our own weakness and our own uncertainty, we know that we cannot be. If we know and trust the one whom we are trying to serve, we know that we need not be.

(*d*) *There cannot be 'a' Christian politics or economics*

Thus it emerges fairly clearly that there cannot be 'a' Christian economic or political programme, to be contrasted with secular or non-Christian ones. Attempts in some countries to set up Christian political parties, or to advocate certain political views as being especially Christian ones, have only had the effect of discrediting the Christian faith by associating it with particular classes or interests, usually, in practice those of property or business. They have alienated from the church many sincere people who cannot accept the line of policy advocated, or who feel that the name of Christ is being invoked to support what they regard as unjust or untrue.

We will normally expect to see Christians sincerely giving support to a wide range of political and economic views and parties. In the situation in Britain today some will be Conservatives, some Labour and some Liberal, or perhaps Scottish or Welsh Nationalists. Some will feel that private property and private enterprise are essential to a free society and an efficient economy, however much they may be subject to abuses in practice. Others will feel that Christian ideals of justice and equality lead inevitably towards some sort of socialism, even though they will be aware of the dangers of totalitarianism inherent in the extension of State ownership and control.

The situation is not so clear where Christians are faced with regimes which seem clearly to be based on philosophies or ideologies hostile to Christianity. Can we say that there is no one Christian position towards the State to be adopted, for instance, by those who faced persecution by the Roman Empire, or who had to live under the Nazis in the last generation, or the Communists today? Yet even here we find differences of approach as to how far it is possible to accept and co-operate with a hostile regime, supporting that part of its activities which seem to be good, and where the stand of uncompromising opposition must be made.

But whatever the party or philosophy to which they feel themselves to be attracted, Christians will try never to be uncritical supporters of it. They will realize that no political creed can have a monopoly of the truth, which is much too wide and varied to be so compressed. They will realize that any party, especially if it is in power, has to compromise with the realities of the political situation. This means that it must inevitably modify somewhat the purity of the principles which it professes, but it is always tempted to go further than this. The temptation is to make political necessity the excuse for taking actions which compromise those fundamentals of justice and fair dealing between men and groups which are part and parcel of the implications of Christian truth. Thus there comes a point where Christians, like all men and women of principle, must stand by what they believe even against a party to which they are deeply committed. Christians will thus see their role as being that of giving loyal, but critical, support to any group to which they belong.

Parties and groups, however idealistic and dedicated, tend also to get set in their ways of thinking and acting. The revolutionary ideals of the founders can easily harden into dogmas, especially amid the strains of political conflict. Christians, like other independent thinkers, thus have another critical function, of acting as the leaven by which new vision and new ways of thought can break into the life of the group. The wind of the spirit blows where it lists, challenging set ideas and patterns, and Christians must be ready to be the means by which he can work among the structures of society.

(*e*) *Are there any issues on which Christians will be united?*

Christians will thus tend to be divided in their views on most of the ordinary issues of public life, though they should try to hold these views with charity for and understanding of those who differ from them. Are there nevertheless any issues which cut across the normal political divisions and on which Christians may be expected to take a united stand?

One can think of some issues on which one would expect such a unity in terms of general principle. Opposition to slavery, for instance, or to the use of torture, or arbitrary arrest and imprisonment without proper legal process, or generally legalized euthanasia, might suggest themselves. Opposition to discrimination on grounds of race and colour, or sex, or political and religious opinion, one would imagine would be another such area, though history and current practice reveal, alas, many cases where this has not been so. Different branches of the Christian church have vigorously persecuted one another's adherents through much of history, and Christians in South Africa support apartheid. Another field of common ground should be advocacy of compassionate care for the sick, the poor, the under-privileged and all in need, though here again there has been much disagreement about how this should be expressed in practical policies.

But one has to state the issue in terms as general as these to get any agreement, and once we come down to specific policy questions the disagreements soon begin again. To mention only a few obvious instances, Christians are divided on abortion law reform, on capital punishment, on how to deal with crime in general, most strikingly on whether the use of military force is justified. One must conclude that in societies such as ours, permeated with centuries of Christian and humanitarian thinking, the practical issues on which all, or even most, Christians will find themselves united against non-Christians, are very few indeed. But that this might not be true of Christians living under openly non-Christian regimes we can also see from examples ranging from the Roman Empire in the first few centuries up to the Communist regimes of today.

Our conclusion must be, therefore, that there is not 'a' Christian economic or political philosophy in the same sense that we can say that there is a Marxist one, or a scientific one, in spite of the many different brands of Marxism or of scientific humanism. This is perhaps not surprising when we come back to the point from which we began, namely that Christianity is fundamentally a matter of a relationship to a person, rather than the acceptance of a system of beliefs. It has about it a freedom and a spontaneity which cannot be confined within the bounds of theoretical systems. It can embrace men and women who find intellectual satisfaction in a wide variety of such systems, but it will transcend all of them. The distinctiveness of the Christian approach is thus one of attitude rather than of theory. It implies accepting people as people, whatever their circumstances, because it arises out of the belief that God so accepts them.

Having thus discussed in general terms the ways in which Christians are likely to approach economic and political problems in the light of their beliefs, we now proceed to illustrate these more fully and draw out their implications more deeply by looking at some of the practical problems of our day. And first of all, because of its crucial importance to our well being and the way in which it dominates the scene in the mid '70s, we look in chapter 3 at the problem of inflation.

3

Inflation

1. *What is inflation?*

The metaphor of inflation is of course derived from the blowing up of a balloon or a tyre. When you blow air into a balloon, the fabric stretches and becomes taut, without the original shell becoming any bigger. Similarly, if you pump money into an economy, so that the money supply grows faster than the capacity to increase the real output of goods and services, prices of all kinds will tend to rise. When the money supply is reduced at a faster rate than capacity, prices should tend to fall.

In practice it is not quite as simple as this. It is true that the most characteristic symptom of inflation is rising prices, but the relationship between the price level and the volume of money is not as straightforward as the metaphor implies. In a deflationary situation, in the short run at least, unemployment of labour and under-used plant and factories are more conspicuous than falling prices. In fact, prices may continue to rise.

(*a*) *The interaction between demand and capacity*

A great deal depends on the level of demand in the economy relative to the underlying productive capacity. That is to say, it is a question of how much we are trying to get out in terms of the goods and services we want to use, relative to what can be produced.

At any time the country has the capacity to produce a fairly closely defined range of volumes of output. There is a labour force of a certain size, with a given number of workers with different types of skills and experience. There are so many coal miners, farmers, bricklayers, fitters, foremen, factory managers, teachers, doctors, civil servants and so on. Their numbers change only slowly, as more young people join the labour force, or as people switch from one job to another, which will involve retraining. Similarly there is a certain amount of productive capital, factories, houses, roads, power stations, vehicles, machines, tools and so on, and a certain level of stocks of raw materials, semi-finished and finished goods. These can be augmented to some extent by selling exports in order to pay for imports of goods which cannot be produced so cheaply at home. Stocks can be built up or run down. Fixed capital can be changed, but more slowly, as new buildings are put up and new plant installed, or old ones pulled down or scrapped.

The underlying productive capacity thus tends to grow and change, but only relatively slowly. The use we try to make of it is more volatile. Demand for the goods and services which the economy produces is apt to fluctuate considerably. Though the long run trend is normally upwards, there is usually a cyclical pattern, with demand and hence output rising faster than underlying capacity during boom periods, and rising more slowly or even falling during periods of recession or slump.

During the post-war period up to the early seventies these cycles were short and slight, lasting only about four or five years. In Britain, for instance, up to 1974, national output has tended to grow in real terms at an average rate of 2 to $2\frac{1}{2}$% a year. The annual rate has been as high as 4 to 5% in boom years and has fallen to nil or very occasionally been negative in years of recession. The biggest single factor affecting the timing of the cycle in Britain has been government policy, in the form of what has come to be called stop-go. During periods of expansion, imports have risen faster than exports, the balance of payments has been threatened and the government has pursued deflationary fiscal and monetary policies to protect the foreign exchange reserves. These have damped down economic activity, curbed imports and cured the drain on the exchange, but in time have led to a rise in unemployment. The government has countered this by pursuing a 'go' policy of using fiscal and monetary policy to expand demand again, output has risen but imports have once again risen faster and so the cycle recurs.

Once an upward or downward movement of demand starts, it tends to become cumulative. Spending of money by consumers buying goods, business men carrying out investment, the government expanding public services, or foreigners buying our exports, creates incomes for those who make and sell goods and services. The people who receive increased income in turn spend most of the extra on other goods and services and this in turn creates further incomes and so a movement of expansion spreads throughout the economy as unemployed labour and capital are brought into use and output is increased, with what is known as a multiplier effect. Similarly with a downward movement, if spending is contracted, this reduces other people's incomes and hence induces them to cut their spending, with a cumulative downward multiplier effect on incomes and production.

As output and incomes grow during the expansion phase, at first there is plenty of unused capacity to draw on. Men are unemployed, plant is idle and there are large stocks of materials and components. After a time, however, bottlenecks begin to appear. Certain types of skilled labour, or materials, or components, become scarce, and pressure of demand for them forces up wages and prices. If demand continues to grow faster than underlying capacity, the supply of unused resources begins to dry up. It cannot be increased quickly since it takes time to train men for new jobs or to build new plant. If demand pressure continues, therefore, it will force up prices and this in turn will lead to further price rises. Firms will pay higher wages to get scarce labour and higher prices for scarce materials. Those who receive higher incomes will want to spend them. This will mean that demand is buoyant and that higher costs can be passed on to the public in the form of higher prices. The cost of living thus goes up and this leads to demands for further pay increases to keep pace, and so we have the familiar price-wage spiral.

In the downswing, on the other hand, prices tend to be relatively sticky. When demand falls off and firms find unsold goods piling up, they are reluctant at first to cut their prices and so make losses. Workers are concerned to protect their living standards and resist wage cuts, the more so as the cost of living is not falling, but often still rising. Thus the recession tends to show up in a rise in unemployment and short-time working and other forms of under-use of capacity, rather than in a fall in prices. In fact, in the post-war period, when up till now recessions have been mild, the general level of prices has rarely if ever fallen.

(b) The role of money

Where does the money supply come into this picture? Of course, in the expansion phase, the money supply must increase to make possible the rise in incomes and the increased value of transactions as output grows. If firms could not get credit from the banks, they would not be able to meet their bills for wages and materials. They would be forced to cut back on production. The government can in fact control the money supply through their short term borrowing by means of Treasury Bills and similar securities, which the banks hold as reserves against their liabilities to depositors. If the banks' reserves of such bills are increased, this makes it possible for them to expand their loans to customers and these loans in turn are spent by the borrowers and reappear as additional deposits in the banks. Thus the government can make possible cumulative expansions and contractions of the money supply through their control over the banks' reserves.[1]

But the money supply is not a fixed entity. Nowadays the bulk of it consists of bank deposits, with notes and coins merely acting as small change. But in addition to current account deposits which can be drawn on freely by cheque, there are also deposit accounts, or time deposits as the Americans call them. These earn interest and hence are used as a store of liquid funds, but they can be withdrawn and spent at short notice. There are other assets, like deposits with building societies and hire-purchase finance companies, which are rather less liquid, but still can be fairly easily withdrawn. These institutions use their deposits to make loans for the purchase of houses on mortgage, or the hire-purchase of cars and other consumer durables. They can thus be the means of enabling money that would otherwise be idle to change hands more freely.

Thus the effective money supply depends not only on the volume of what is officially recorded as money, such as cash and bank deposits, but also on how quickly it turns over. At times of active business expansion, the volume of transactions can grow faster than the money supply, as people tend to transfer their money from bank deposits where it earns little or no return, to deposits with other institutions which will pay higher interest rates and also set it actively to work through their loans to those who can use it. They will also themselves make loans to industry and commerce. At times when business is slack and people are more concerned with safety, they may be less willing to take such risks and leave their money idle in banks.

Thus the essence of inflation is much more complex than a straightforward relationship between the quantity of money and the level of prices. It involves also both the level of activity in the economy relative to its underlying productive capacity, and also the extent to which a given money supply can be turned over more quickly or more slowly to finance a given volume of transactions.

Traditionally, this was expressed in the formula by which Irving Fisher[2] summed up the so-called Quantity Theory of Money:

$$MV = PT$$

—where M stands for the quantity of money, V the velocity of circulation (or speed at which it turns over), P the general price level and T the volume of transactions.

As it stands, this expression is a mere identity. It does not imply any particular causal relationship between the four variables, but it does serve to bring together and focus the interrelations which we have been considering. For instance, during the early part of a period of expansion, when demand and output are rising, but there are unused resources, M and V may be increasing, but T will also be increasing as output grows, so P may remain unchanged. Once resources begin to get scarce, if demand still rises and M is still increasing, then T will no longer rise proportionately and P will begin to rise. On the other hand, a rise in M may be offset by a fall in V, as would happen during a slump, when attempts to encourage expansion by increasing the money supply would be frustrated because the extra money would tend to get absorbed into idle deposits because the public regard it as too risky to lend it to industry which in any case may be unwilling to borrow and spend it. In other circumstances an expansion of output can take place with little increase in M, if V is rising, through liquid deposits being activated by being lent to financial institutions which set them to work through loans. Something of this sort happened in the 1950s, when there was inflationary pressure, but little rise in measurable money supply, because idle deposits accumulated during the war were being actively lent out by hire purchase finance companies and similar bodies.

2. *Inflation as we have experienced it in practice*

So much for the theory of inflation. As a practical experience it has become only too familiar throughout most of the world in recent decades. In Britain, for instance, over the twenty years 1950–51 to 1970–71, the retail price index rose annually by amounts varying from 1 to 9½% with an overall average of a little under 4%. The annual price rises were higher in periods of expansion, ranging up to 6 or 8% on average, but only about 1 or 2% in years of stagnation.

More recently, since about 1968, the rate of price rise has steepened, especially in the last few years. In 1972–73 the retail price index rose by nearly 10% and in the twelve months to July 1975 by no less than 26%.[3] The reasons for this acceleration must be discussed more fully later, but it was clearly associated with the very steep rise in world primary commodity prices, including those of oil, and also with attempts by income receivers to keep up with previous rises in the cost of living by pressing for higher increases of pay.

Inflation is a world-wide phenomenon. Until recently Britain's record was certainly no worse than that of comparable countries and better than that of, say, France or Italy. In the last few years, however, Britain has been more severely affected than many of her neighbours. Over the year from spring 1974 to spring 1975, for instance, the index of consumer prices went up by the following percentages:

Percentage rise of consumer prices 1974–75

United States	10·3
Canada	11·3
Japan	14·2
France	13·5
West Germany	5·9
Italy	20·3
United Kingdom	21·2

(*National Institute Economic Review*, May 1975, table 4, p. 31)

By the spring of 1975, Britain's rate of inflation was the highest among the countries quoted. Moreover, whereas in most of the main industrial countries the rate of inflation was now declining, though at the cost of a steep rise in unemployment, in Britain it was accelerating, though unemployment was still considerably lower.

Inflation is, of course, not new. Over the centuries, the trend of prices has been upwards, though this has sometimes been interrupted by fairly long periods of generally falling prices, as between 1815 and about 1850, and between the mid-1870s and the mid-1890s and again from 1920 to 1933. International trade and financial networks ensure that these trends are transmitted fairly generally throughout the world.

The long periods of upward trends of prices in the past have been associated with increases in the world's money supply arising from large-scale gold discoveries. They have also been associated with periods of large-scale technological development and heavy investment, which have increased the demands made on productive resources and have led to rising money incomes, but have only produced the fruits of increased supplies of cheaper consumer goods after a delay. But inflation as we have known it in recent decades has been at a faster rate than that found during such past periods of price rise. Nevertheless we can distinguish several distinct types of case, and it will help us to clearer understanding if we look at them more closely. In descending order of steepness of price rise they are as follows:[4]

(a) Hyperinflation

By this we mean a situation where the money supply rises so fast that the public lose confidence in money as a store of value. This results in a rocketing of prices as buyers seek to get rid of money for goods as soon as they get it. The price index can multiply by thousands, or even millions, in the course of a year. Classical examples are the German inflation of 1922–23 and the Hungarian and Chinese inflations of 1945–48, while in Germany after 1945 official prices did not rise, but money virtually ceased to be used and recourse was made to more acceptable media such as cigarettes to get hold of the small supply of goods available. Earlier historical cases are those of the French assignats during the Revolution of the 1790s and American greenbacks during the Civil War of 1861–65.

Such hyperinflation typically arises out of a war situation, when normal production is interrupted and the supply of goods to consumers drastically reduced. Governments resort to the printing press to meet their urgent need to spend on defence and other public services, since they are often unable to get hold of the resources they need by taxation or borrowing from the public, or by the use of direct controls. In particular, in the dislocation which arises at the end of an unsuccessful war, the temptation is strong to pump out money to keep men employed, irrespective of whether there is anything to spend it on. Eventually the monetary system collapses completely, and a new monetary unit has to be introduced, but not until savings have been wiped out and those whose incomes cannot keep pace with the astronomical rise in prices have been ruined, while speculators who can take advantage of the price rises can make fantastic profits.

(b) Strato-inflation

This term has been applied to a situation which has existed in some countries, especially in Latin America, but also in parts of the Middle and Far East. Prices have tended over the years to rise steeply, at annual rates varying from 20% up to 100 or 200% or sometimes more, but confidence in the monetary system has never broken down enough to lead to runaway hyperinflation. The origin of the rapid rise once again is usually large-scale deficit spending by the government, often on carrying out rapid development programmes, building roads, railways and power supplies and giving lavish aid to industrialization but also on paying a large force of public servants. Such countries have often been dependent on the export of a few staple agricultural or mineral products and have suffered from a slump in their export prices. Hence they have tended to go in for elaborate structures of import and export licensing and exchange controls. These have allowed their internal prices to go on rising without a catastrophic loss of foreign exchange reserves.

Financial institutions in such countries are often weak, so that the effects of large-scale deficit spending soon get out of hand. Social structures are rigid and incomes very unequal, so that the lower paid are striving to get a fairer share as well as to keep up with rising prices. To ease the social and political tensions, inflation tends to be institutionalized. Thus wage and salary rates and social security payments are made to increase regularly with the cost of living index, while the capital values of assets such as loans and shares are similarly indexed so that they keep up with rising prices. Thus money interest rates can be kept at realistic levels and an incentive is given to saving.

In spite of these adaptations to inflation as a way of life, political and social strains and stresses have continued in most of these countries. Authoritarian regimes have been common, often following a breakdown of democratic government as in Brazil, Argentina, Chile and Uruguay.

(*c*) *Chronic inflation*

This is perhaps a more apt description of what has been found in most of the free market economies in the last two decades. As in Britain and Western Europe, prices have risen steadily at annual rates varying from 1 or 2% a year in periods of slack trade, up to 7 to 10% in years of rapid growth. Until recently the annual rise has rarely exceeded 10% and has normally been checked, but not reversed, by government deflationary policies.

The generally high and growing level of world trade has spread inflation from one country to another, for rapid growth and rising prices in one country have attracted imports from others, while rising costs of exports have spread price rises to other countries. Until recently, however, the system of fixed exchange rate parities between countries tended to act as a check on inflation. Countries where price rises went ahead too fast tended to suffer from balance of payments deficits, since high prices checked the demand for their exports and sucked in imports. In order to protect their reserves, governments were then forced to deflate their internal demand, by increasing taxes, curbing public spending and restricting credit and the money supply. This usually served to slow down the rise in prices by creating unemployment. However, the rapid general rise in world trade and incomes, and the desire of governments to avoid large-scale unemployment, meant that deflation was not usually pursued for very long, so that the rise in prices tended to be slowed down rather than stopped, to pick up again once the expansion of the economy got under way again.

Why has inflation got so much steeper in the last few years? This we must look at in more detail later on, but some general reasons can be given here.

First, the breakdown of the Bretton Woods[5] system of fixed parities between different national currencies left governments freer to disregard balance of payments deficits and continue expansionary policies, since their currencies could be allowed to float downwards without loss of reserves, or could be more easily devalued if deficits arose.

Secondly, the years 1972–73 were marked by very rapid growth in output and incomes in the main industrial countries and this set up a steeply rising demand for primary products such as foodstuffs, raw materials and fuels. The pressure of demand, together with harvest failure for certain crops like wheat, maize and soya beans, and the running down of American reserve stocks, as well as the decision of the oil producing countries to raise their prices fourfold, together lay behind the general explosion of primary product prices in 1973–74. This in turn led to a steep rise in the cost of living which consumers could not ignore. Once wage and salary earners have experienced a rise in living costs of 10% or more, they naturally tend to anticipate this in their claims for higher pay, so that cost inflation due to rising food and raw material prices comes to be reinforced by cost inflation due to higher labour costs, as employers seek to pass on their higher costs in still further price increases. We must therefore raise the question whether these are merely temporary difficulties, to be overcome by wise policy, or whether they indicate a development of chronic inflation into strato-inflation.

(*d*) *Suppressed inflation*

Finally, we must consider cases where inflationary pressure exists, but where controls over the use of resources prevent it finding more than limited expression in the form of rising prices.

This happened, for instance, in Britain during the Second World War. The need to divert manpower and materials and plant away from meeting civilian consumption led to growing inflationary pressure, since those employed on war production were receiving incomes and there was little to spend on. But the pressure was largely suppressed through increased taxation and savings drives to absorb spending power, and by physical controls over the use of materials and labour together with consumer rationing. Prices rose, but not very steeply.

In the centrally planned economies of Eastern Europe the position is similar. Although in varying degrees elements of the market have been reintroduced, with enterprises now being freer to fix their output and adapt their prices to changes in costs and in demand, yet it remains true that the basic decisions concerning what is to be produced and at what prices it is to be sold are still taken by administrative decree. General price levels have in fact remained very stable in these countries over the years. Yet inflationary pressure has not been absent. Partly this is because the supply of consumer goods and services has never kept up with the rise in incomes. To some extent this is the result of deliberate policy, in giving priority to the capital investment needed for large-scale industrialization. In part it is due to inefficiencies in the structure, in particular to the failure of the agricultural section to meet its planned output targets, but also to a lack of concern for adequate provision for consumer services like retailing, catering and household repairs. There is also the fact that, though wage rates are centrally fixed, earnings are not, since they depend very largely on payment by results through piece rates and bonuses. Thus a good deal of pressure of unsatisfied demand builds up but it is reflected in empty shelves in shops and queues for available supplies, rather than in price rises.

3. *The factors lying behind the present inflationary situation*

We have seen that the situation in the main industrial countries over the last twenty years has been one of slow, but chronic, inflation, but that more recently the pace of inflation has quickened and there are fears that this acceleration may become self-reinforcing. We need now to look more closely at some of the factors lying behind this acceleration.

(*a*) *How far demand-pull and how far cost-push?*

We saw above the essential part played in inflation by excess demand, with income receivers trying to get more out of the economy than its productive capacity can supply, and thus forcing prices up. The process of chronic inflation was started off in the early post-war period by demand-pull influences of this sort, because spending power was then swollen by wartime savings and by the continued high level of employment, but there were still shortages of most types of goods. Demand-pull was also characteristic of periods of boom in the post-war cycles, when expansionary fiscal and monetary policies encourage growth of production and income and hence of demand, but the flow of consumer goods on to the markets tends to lag behind.

Can the same be said of recession periods like 1962–63, 1971–72, or 1974–75, when unemployment was rising to levels unprecedentedly high by post-war standards and firms were working below capacity, and yet money incomes and prices continued to rise? Must we not maintain that in such circumstances demand-pull has given way to cost-push, and that we must look for explanation to institutional factors such as trade union power, or psychological factors such as changed expectations by employees and employers? Similarly, in 1972–73 the steep world-wide rise in primary product prices and hence in raw material and foodstuff costs was undoubtedly the biggest immediate cause in sparking off the steeper rise of prices which followed.

This is in part a hen and egg problem, for demand-pull and cost-push are always intertwined. Price increases induced by excess demand give rise to pay demands to keep up with living costs. Pay rises in turn both raise money incomes and so keep up demand pressure, and also increase business costs and force firms to seek to pass these on in higher prices.

Why, then, have higher levels of unemployment in recent years, especially during recessions, not curbed the willingness of employees to seek higher pay and of employers to grant it? This is what one would expect once the pressure of excess demand had been removed. A number of reasons can be given for this.

1. First, the published figures of registered unemployment and registered unfilled vacancies are not very accurate indicators of changes in the pressure of demand relative to capacity. Many people who become unemployed do not register at the employment exchange. This applies especially to married women, most of whom are not insured against unemployment in their own right and hence cannot draw benefit. It also affects people over retirement age, who if they become unemployed tend to retire on their pensions. Also, many unfilled vacancies are never notified by the employers to the exchange, especially if there seems little chance of their being filled.

Moreover, the introduction of earnings-related supplements to unemployment benefit in 1966, and of statutory payments by employers to redundant workers in 1965, has somewhat reduced the financial hardship of unemployment, especially to the better paid and more highly skilled. They are perhaps more likely to take a bit longer looking round for a suitable job, rather than take the first thing that comes along.

Among those who are unemployed for longer periods, there is a hard core of older men whose skills or experience have been made obsolete by technical changes, and who have very little chance of getting another job. At the same time, even in times of slack trade, there have been acute shortages of certain types of skills, such as those of building tradesmen and engineering craftsmen. This has been true even in areas of high unemployment like West Central Scotland and North-East England.

All of this suggests that while a national figure of 4% unemployment such as was reached in 1972 is undoubtedly high by post-war standards, the more usual national average of around 2½% which has prevailed since the mid-sixties may not indicate any less pressure of demand in the economy than the 1½% average more common in the fifties and early sixties.

2. Secondly, there is no doubt that the experience of thirty years of almost continuous full employment, with rising prices but also rising real earnings, has had a marked effect on the attitudes of employees. People have come to expect a regular rise in their standard of living and to be disappointed when it is slower than they expect because Britain's real output has been growing more slowly than that of her neighbours.

Experience of rising prices means that the money illusion has gradually been worn away. When prices were rising only 2 or 3% a year, this might be ignored in formulating wage claims, but once people have found that money pay rises have been largely eroded by ever steeper price rises, they begin to expect this to continue. Money pay claims are put in big enough to outstrip the expected rise in the cost of living. When this gets into double figures, the cumulative effect on pay claims speeds up faster.

Along with this goes the vexed issue of comparability. Most groups of workers tend to compare their rates of pay with other groups, sometimes those who are thought to be doing work of comparable skill or status, sometimes those whose skills or status they regard as superior or inferior. If semi-skilled workers have had a rise, craftsmen must have one to keep up differentials. Locomotive drivers feel that they ought to have a differential over signalmen or guards, but the latter feel that they ought to keep up with the loco men. Teachers feel their position threatened when men and women without their professional training and responsibilities overtake them in pay levels. Always, there is some comparable group which has just had a rise, so we must have one too.

3. Thirdly, a rise in trade union militancy is often quoted as another factor underlying cost-push inflation. It is doubtful how far this is a

separate cause. Trade unions are stronger under some historical conditions than in others, and in some occupations than in others. The prevalence of full employment has undoubtedly given them greater power, and so has the trend towards larger scale business and commercial units, which makes it easier to organize. But the amount of support which unions get, and the amount of rank and file militancy among their members, are very much the result of the extent to which the members feel they have grievances which warrant industrial action, and the extent to which they feel that such action is likely to be successful. Some occupations, like those of the miners and the dockers, have long traditions of militancy for historical reasons, but overall it is not surprising to find more militancy in the situation of the 1970s than there was in the 1930s, or even in the late forties and early fifties, when people had large amounts of wartime savings to spend and prices were not rising as fast as they are today.

4. Fourthly, there has also been another specific factor which has intensified the pressure in recent years. Not only have increases in money earnings been largely swallowed up by rising prices, but also by increased income tax payments. The income threshold at which tax liability begins has not been raised to keep pace with the fall in the value of money, so that liability now begins much lower down the relative income scale than it did. In the early seventies, even though the threshold was lifted somewhat in the 1972 Budget, we had the paradoxical situation that a man receiving family income supplement because his earnings were deemed to be too low for adequate support of his family could also be paying income tax. This added to the feeling that you had to run ever faster in terms of money income to stay where you were.

5. Fifthly, employers' expectations have also changed over the years, making them more willing to grant pay increases. The long continuance of full employment and rising prices has led to a presumption that it will normally be possible to pass on higher labour costs through higher prices and still be able to sell the product. For many large firms in industries like motor manufacturing, electronics or chemicals, it is so important to keep plant worth millions of pounds in operation that it is worth paying higher wage rates to avoid the overheads piling up on an idle plant. Such firms are more concerned with long-term prospects, looking several years ahead, than they are with prices in the next few months, and this is the more true of the large multinational companies, for whom to have a plant idle in Britain may hold up the flow of components to other plant all over the world.

Moreover, about a quarter of the manpower of the country is now employed in the public sector, taking together the central and local governments, services like education and the National Health Service, and the nationalized industries. In the case of the nationalized industries, whether they can grant pay increases depends more on whether the government will let them put up prices, or will give them a subsidy if they make losses, than on strict considerations of commercial viability. Since they provide essential services like power and transport, the pressure to give increases of pay to avoid a stoppage is very great. In the case of non-commercial staffs in the public sector, such as civil servants, teachers, doctors and nurses, local government officers or cleansing workers, the decision to pay or not to pay higher rates of salaries and wages is even more purely political, since they have to be met either out of taxation or through credit creation. Again, since these are essential services, the pressure to pay more is strong, though not always successful: witness the case of the postal workers in 1971.

6. We may conclude that cost-pull factors in our recent inflation have been strong, especially the steep rise in primary product prices in 1973–74 and the wage-price spiral which was accelerated by it. Its effect in Britain was made worse by the downward drifting of the floating pound which further put up our import prices. Nevertheless, though unemployment has been higher than in earlier post-war years and the pressure of acute excess demand less evident, yet it is probably still true that there is a demand-pull basis to the cost-push pressure. Present demand, and more important expected demand, have not yet fallen enough to alter employers' willingness to grant increases rather than face prolonged strikes, and employees' willingness to press for them without fear of unemployment. No doubt, if unemployment was to rise far enough, it would halt this process, but evidence suggests that to change expectations it would have to rise much higher than we have so far been prepared to envisage. Perhaps to the two or three millions experienced in the early thirties.

(*b*) *The monetarist argument*

The above analysis is along the lines that would have been accepted by most economists and politicians until recently. In the last few years, however, there has been a revival of the monetarist argument, namely the control of the rate of growth of the money supply is the key factor in the regulation of the economy.

According to this line of thought, pressure by trade unions and other groups of workers for more pay should not be regarded as the chief causal factor in the recent inflationary spiral. Workers are only reacting to rises in the cost of living made possible by the government's expansion of the money supply through its own deficit spending, which injects demand into the economy and so bids up the prices of scarce labour and other resources. If the growth in the money supply had been restrained, firms would have been unable to pay higher wages, because they could not get bank loans, or if they did pay them, they would have had to lay off workers. Increased pay in the public sector would also have been impossible, if the government had not been prepared to create the spending power, or at least, it would have had to be balanced by increased taxation, which would have withdrawn spending power proportionately.

It is certainly true that the very large increases in government spending in 1971 and 1972, designed to secure a breakthrough into faster growth, did involve massive rises in the money supply and led to demands on scarce resources of skilled labour, components and supplies of all sorts which both encourage pressure for higher wages and sucked in imports on a large scale to make up for the failure of home production to rise fast enough. Moreover, the government has had a 'net borrowing requirement' or deficit of spending over tax revenue, in every year since 1962–63, apart from 1968–69 and 1969–70, at the height of Mr Jenkins' deflationary policy following devaluation. By 1974–75 this had risen to £7,500 million out of a total public expenditure of £44,000 million.[6] But this was also the period when primary product prices began their steep rise on world markets.

To some extent this is a circular argument. No one denies that the pressure of demand against capacity, the effect of increased costs of imported primary products and of rising wages, and changes in both the supply of money and its velocity of circulation, are all involved in the process of inflation. In 1972–74 world primary product prices were rising, imparting a sharp upward thrust to the cost of living. Workers were pressing for higher pay, both to keep up with the cost of living and because they aspired to higher real incomes. The government was spending more relative to its tax revenue, partly because unemployment was still high, partly to try to achieve a breakthrough to a higher rate of growth, and partly because of long run upward trends of commitments to spend on education, health and welfare services, social security, housing, roads, aid to ailing industries and regions, and many other things.

Faced with such a situation, could the money supply have been curbed? Only if the government had been prepared to allow unemployment to rise, so that employers could no longer pass on pay increases, and workers gave up pressing for them. Only if they had also been prepared to curb spending on better schools and more teachers, improved hospitals, welfare services for the aged and disabled, higher pensions, the building of roads, housing and aid to industry in the development areas. Or if they had been prepared to finance such spending by higher taxation, which would have withdrawn spending power from the economy and so caused higher unemployment.

There thus has to be a trade off between alternative objectives. How important are stable prices as an object of policy, as compared with maintaining full employment, or greater social justice through improved social services, or investment to improve the efficiency of industry?

Inflation is undoubtedly an evil, once it rises above a low level. It destroys confidence in money and discourages saving. It redistributes income unfairly, benefiting those who can keep up with it by making profits out of price rises, or by having the bargaining power to secure pay increases, at the expense of those less favourably placed. These include many lower paid workers with little bargaining power, retired persons living on fixed incomes, and old age pensioners unless pensions are adjusted frequently to keep up with price rises. If we experience faster inflation than our competitors, it makes it difficult for us to sell our exports and so pay for our imports.

But how far are we prepared to go to avoid these evils, if the only way to do so is to restrict the money supply so as to bring about unemployment on the scale of the thirties, or to curb public spending so that pensioners must remain in poverty or school children have a worse chance of a decent education? In particular, once a steep rise in prices had already taken place through the effects of the rise in primary product prices, it would have been impossible to undo this rise by restricting the money supply without plunging the country into a full-scale depression, which would have led not only to great hardship, but probably to political unrest on a scale which no government could contemplate.

The monetarist answer would be that large-scale unemployment is inevitable anyhow, unless inflation is curbed, because of the balance of payments. Leaving aside the oil deficit, as being on a scale too large to be tackled except by international action, a country which allows inflation to continue unchecked risks finding its exports becoming uncompetitive because of higher costs, while the rise of money incomes will draw in imports. A time will come when it will no longer be able to pay for imports on the scale necessary to maintain full employment. If in such circumstances it fails to deflate, but tries to maintain full employment by running a budget deficit, this will reduce confidence in international financial circles, and they will no longer be willing to hold its currency, or to grant it short term loans to tide over a balance of payments deficit. If it allows its currency to float downwards against other currencies, this may not solve the problem, for it will make its imports even more costly in terms of foreign exchange, and this may outweigh any stimulus to its exports which depreciation gives by making them cheaper to foreign buyers.

So far, Britain's well-developed international banking system, and the prospects of North Sea oil being available in large quantities by 1980, have meant that we have had no difficulty in covering our huge balance of payments deficit by borrowing from abroad, but if confidence in our financial stability became undermined, we should no longer be able to do this.

4. *Policies to deal with inflation*

In a situation like this, what instruments of policy are open to the government? We consider three possible lines, fiscal and monetary policy, prices and incomes policy and acceptance of inflation and adaptation to it.

(*a*) *Fiscal and monetary policy*

A government in a position like that which faced the main industrial countries in 1975 has to walk a knife edge between opposite dangers. The low level of business confidence, the threat of rising unemployment and the dangers of world slump would suggest a policy of reflation, reducing taxes, increasing public expenditure and making money freely available. But this will encourage the already high rate of inflation by keeping up demand and making it easier to grant pay increases, and besides it may make a bad balance of payments situation worse. If on the other hand the emphasis is placed on checking inflation, this would imply a deflationary policy, of higher taxes, lower public spending and dearer and scarcer money. But this will bring many firms to bankruptcy and push up unemployment, and while it will help the balance of payments by checking imports, it will also hit other countries' exports and thus may help to precipitate the threatened world slump.

A straightforward fiscal and monetary policy as indicated by the simple Keynesian model[7] is thus no longer applicable to a complex situation of inflation combined with stagnation. Even the most convinced monetarists, though they would want the money supply restrained and the government's borrowing requirements reduced, would agree that one cannot reverse a rate of inflation like that prevailing in 1975 easily and simply. The aim must be to hold the economy more or less in balance, but there will be disagreement on which side the balance should be tilted. Those who feel that mass unemployment is the greater danger will want to tilt it slightly on the side of reflation; those who stress the greater danger of runaway inflation and balance of payments collapse will want to lean slightly on the side of deflation.

Measures should probably be selective rather than general. Help must be given to industry, to make up for the squeeze on its cash flow arising from higher raw material prices and higher wages, and to give some incentives to the investment on which we rely to get a rise in output and productivity. Help must be given to those groups most affected by rising prices, such as pensioners and those with large families. Such help involves injections of spending power, but seeks to concentrate them where they are most needed. Similarly, there must be countervailing measures to check excess purchasing power and restrict imports, but these again must be selective. Thus in the Budget of April 1975, the Chancellor was obliged to raise taxes and curb expenditure in order to reduce the country's dependence on foreign borrowing. To shield the least well off, he increased the standard rates of income tax, but also put up the allowances so as to raise the threshold. Instead of raising the general rate of VAT, he introduced a higher rate of 25% on luxuries.

There is an obvious dilemma in the use of indirect tax rises, or price increases in nationalized industries. These are demand-deflationary, absorbing purchasing power which cannot be spent on other things, but cost-inflationary, since they put up the cost of living. There must therefore be a careful balancing of their overall effects.

(b) Prices and incomes policy

If it is no longer possible to hold the balance between the capacity of the economy and the demands upon it by fiscal and monetary policy, attention is naturally turned to direct controls over prices and incomes. It would seem only sensible to restrict the giving of pay increases which exceed the likely growth of real output, and to discourage pay claims by restricting the passing on of higher labour costs in higher prices.

Such policies have been common in many countries and have taken many forms. They may involve simple agreements to restrain pay claims within certain limits, as in Britain in 1948–50, and in 1965, or the social contract of 1974, or the £6 a week limit on increases proposed in the summer of 1975. Or they may include more elaborate procedures for the vetting of pay and price increases according to stipulated principles, as in the prices and incomes policies of the Labour government of 1965–70 and of the Conservatives in 1972–74, or in that of the Nixon administration in the United States in 1971–72. Or again they may be intended to provide for the orderly and planned working out of pay increases on a more permanent basis as was done in the Netherlands in the early post-war years, and as is done in Sweden by permanent consultation between the central trade union and employers' organizations.

Where such policies have been introduced as temporary measures in an emergency, they have usually succeeded in bringing about a slowing down of pay and price increases, and in particular a complete freeze for a limited period has often been effective. But pressure for increases built up during their operation has usually led to an explosion of larger claims and grants once the restrictions are removed.

Attempts to work out and apply more permanent policies have been less successful. It has been difficult to reconcile all the different pressures which arise. Pay changes are needed to attract labour into occupations which are short staffed, to meet the needs of those in low paid jobs, to satisfy claims based on established differentials and comparabilities, to give incentives to accept changes in working methods resulting in greater productivity, to keep up with the cost of living. Rates of pay are at one and the same time the price of labour of different degrees of skill and experience, the incomes on which the welfare of families depends, and badges of status reflecting the social valuation of different occupations. There are bound to be conflicts between these functions.

Price controls are equally difficult to apply. They involve the danger of either being so loose as to be ineffective, or so tight as to cause serious problems of lack of funds to firms faced with cost rises.

In a market economy, which depends for its efficient working on flexible prices, permanent and detailed control of prices and incomes is probably an unworkable ideal. Yet the income and price system which prevails is full of anomalies and injustices. The experience of the National Board for Prices and Incomes in the years 1966–70 showed that there was a place for a body prepared to investigate particular cases, expose the facts and try to work out principles on which a more rational system could be based.

Moreover, once a situation of cost inflation and wage-price spiral becomes established, it is no longer practicable to rely on a completely uncontrolled system of market determined incomes and prices. There must be some attempt at control, preferably by voluntary agreement, but if this fails, by statutory authority. Otherwise there must be either escalating inflation, or else a degree of fiscal and monetary deflation adequate to check it by inducing heavy unemployment.

Yet there must be two strong provisos. First, no prices and incomes policy has any chance of success unless it finds general understanding and acceptance. In the last resort, in a free society, it is not possible to stop a powerful group which controls a key source of labour from getting its way, except at the cost of disruption and hardship which the community is not prepared to accept. The example of the miners in recent years has made this clear. The problem is to gain a degree of understanding and acceptance that restraint is necessary in their own ultimate interests as well as those of the community, which will carry conviction to groups with a strong sense of past grievance who feel themselves in a position to get what they feel to be justice.

Secondly, any success which such a policy can have will only be partial. Everyone may admit in theory that it is nonsense to pay ourselves 30% more in money terms when real output has only gone up 1 or 2%, or not at all. Yet when faced with steep rises in the cost of living and all the anomalies caused by other groups getting pay rises, it is not easy to expect groups of workers at any level to put the vague and general interest of the community before their own immediate pockets. Hence no policy is in practice going to be able to prevent all increases in pay or prices which are outside the prescribed norms, but if it succeeds in slowing down the rate of increase and steering the actions of employees and firms in the desired direction, it may be regarded as worth while.

(*c*) *Acceptance of inflation*

A third possibility is often suggested. Why not accept inflation as a way of life? If the results of trying to stop it are either to allow the economy to get into a state of unemployment and under-use of capacity which is highly wasteful, causes great hardship and leads to political tensions, or to override free collective bargaining and market pricing by a system of ever more rigorous and inflexible controls, might it not be better to learn to live with inflation as a lesser evil, and adapt our institutions to cope with it?

It is argued that many of the injustices and inconveniences of inflation can be counteracted by indexation, that is by adjusting various key prices automatically in line with changes in the cost of living index. Thus wage and salary rates would be adjusted proportionately at regular intervals as the cost of living index rose, and so would the rates of retirement pensions and other social security benefits. This would greatly reduce the injustice at present arising from the fact that some groups can protect themselves because they make profits from higher prices, or because they have strong bargaining power, while others, whose bargaining power is weak, or who live on fixed incomes, tend to lose.

Indexation would also be applied to the capital value of all forms of security and other financial assets. Thus the capital value of a government bond, or a company debenture, or a deposit with a bank or a building society, would go up regularly with the cost of living. This would prevent the rate of interest on such assets having to rise to exorbitant heights, to compensate for the fall in their real value as prices rise, and avoid a negative real rate of return on them. At present, a man purchasing an asset valued at £1,000 finds that if the general price level is rising at, say, 20% a year, not only is the real capital value of his asset falling, but the interest he gets will not even give him a return which outstrips this, unless it rises above 20%. There is thus no incentive to put savings into financial assets and thus lend one's money to those who could make productive use of it. Indexation would restore the incentive to save and enable companies and the government to borrow more easily the capital they need.

The cash allowances set against income for income tax purposes would also have to be indexed in the same way, if the problem of falling tax thresholds is to be overcome.

Indexation may well be needed as a practical measure in a situation where inflation has got above the 'chronic' level of up to 10% annually and has entered the 'strato' level of over 20%. For instance, if wages and salaries were pegged to the cost of living index, it might then be practicable to limit severely any pay increases beyond this level. Should this be accepted, it would be hoped that a fall in the price of imported foodstuffs and raw material would gradually slow up the rise in the cost of living, so that the spiral of wages and prices could be wound down. Thus indexation could be an instrument to be used along with others, such as some form of prices and incomes policy and a selective fiscal and monetary policy.

Many would argue that a slow rate of inflation, such as we had in the twenty years up to the mid-sixties, was a price worth paying in order to maintain full employment and free collective bargaining. Yet this is far from saying that inflation at annual rates of 20% upwards is to be regarded as acceptable, if it can be avoided at anything like a reasonable price.

In the first place indexation, though it mitigates the injustices of inflation, also itself gives a further twist to it. The reduced real spending power of those whose incomes are squeezed by inflation acts as a brake on it by reducing the pressure of demand, though admittedly often at the expense of hardship to those who can least afford it. Moreover, acceptance of inflation in this way and the provision of hedges against it reduces the incentive to take more active and perhaps more unpleasant steps to check it.

Secondly, in a country with a long history of collective bargaining like Britain, and where groups of employees have become used to using industrial action to claim pay increases on grounds of comparability with other groups, or contributions to productivity, it is unlikely that such claims can be prevented even by assuring that pay keeps pace automatically with the cost of living. Some groups are always likely to feel that their initial position is unfair, and that they need more than this to gain their just reward. Some of them are likely to be able to make these claims effective. And indeed we cannot accept as permanently appropriate the wage and salary relativities that happen to exist at any particular time. There must be some provision for adjustments to reflect changes in the demand for and supply of various types of skills, as well as to ensure what is felt to be a socially fair distribution of incomes.

Thirdly, money cannot continue to perform its functions effectively unless its value is reasonably stable. Even though indexation might help to protect the real purchasing power of financial assets, money can perform its function as a store of value better if people can have confidence that £1 today will continue to be something like £1 in its real value next year. Once again, therefore, an ending of inflation, or at least a considerable moderation of it, is preferable to acceptance, provided it can be obtained without too great a social cost.

5. *What light can be thrown on the problem by Christian understanding?*

We have gone at considerable length into an analysis both of the inherent nature of inflation and of the reasons why it has risen to crisis levels in 1974–75. It is essential for Christian men and women to have this sort of understanding if they are to bring the distinctive understanding of human society which arises from their beliefs to bear on such a complex problem. Christians cannot claim to have any mysterious 'Christian solution' which can be brought in where politicians and economists have failed. They can, however, claim there are certain insights, certain ways of looking at things, certain attitudes in the face of challenging situations, which may be helpful. They include the following:

(*a*) *Recognition of unpalatable facts*

As we have already seen, most people would admit objectively, if pressed, that it makes no sense for us to pay ourselves 20% or more in money terms, at a time when the volume of goods and services we can produce is only going up by 2 or 3% at the most, or is even stationary or going down slightly. Yet each group of people feels that its own immediate interests force it to press for such increases, to keep up with the cost of living, or with some comparable group which has already had one.

Christians are no less likely than anyone else to feel concern when their standard of living is threatened by rising prices, or when they see others getting pay rises which they do not get. But they ought to be more ready to question their own motives and assumptions and hence to accept unpleasant truths about the world, even when they go against their own interests. In particular, they should feel compelled to give priority to the interests of the community as a whole, as part of the compulsion to love one's neighbour as oneself. Similarly, they should be able to look at their own standard of living objectively, in comparison with the standards enjoyed by those who are better off, and worse off, than themselves.

(*b*) *Understanding the ways in which the economy works even if we do not approve of them*

A related point to this is that Christians should find it easier to achieve a certain degree of objectivity in understanding the way in which the economy actually works, even if it does not fit into our preconceptions of how things ought to be. For instance, we may look askance at differentials in pay as being contrary to the principle that all men are equal in the sight of God, and yet recognize that if labour is to be steered to those uses in which it is most needed, in an imperfect world where men are selfish as well as altruistic, some differentials are essential to attract workers into expanding occupations and away from contracting ones, as well as to fill jobs which involve greater training or responsibility. Contrariwise, if we are in well-paid jobs of high prestige, and inclined to feel that this is in the nature of things, if we are Christians we shall try to be open to the call from the less privileged to have a more equal share of the world's goods. This is justified by their having needs and seeking opportunities no less urgently than we do.

Similarly, however much our instinct may be to disapprove of profits as a source of inequality in income and power, we will recognize that they have a function in any practicable economic system, as being both an incentive to use resources efficiently and a criterion to judge how far this has been done, and also as a source of saving out of which necessary investment can be carried out. At the same time, if our instinct is to applaud the virtues of profit as a reward for enterprise, we will seek also to be aware of the dangers of the pursuit of profit as an end in itself, and of the need to develop mechanisms to ensure that it is subordinated to the public good.

These issues will be considered more fully in chapter 7, but they are obviously relevant to prices and incomes policy and the need to help industry with its cash flow problems at times of severe inflation.

(*c*) *Recognition and understanding of the aspirations of groups other than our own*

Another contribution which those with Christian experience and understanding ought to be able to bring is a kind of empathy which can enter into and appreciate the feelings and aspirations of groups other than our own.

This is not easy, for most of us are inevitably influenced by the background in which we grow up or live. Whether we like it or not, we are working class or middle class, professional, managerial or operative in our ways of thinking and our accepted values. It requires an effort of sympathy and imagination to transcend this background. But Christians should have both the perspective and the motive to seek to do so, for they believe that all men are God's children, but that all also, including themselves, are fallible and imperfect.

Hence, Christians have a special responsibility to recognize, for instance, that those who have grown up as manual workers in industry, and perhaps been active in trade unions, have a different way of looking at the working of the economy and of society than have those whose experience is in management or business, and that those who are teachers, or academics, or civil servants, will see things differently again. For instance, wage claims by the miners, or the dock workers, look very different to miners or dock workers, with their history of bitter struggles over the decades, than they do to academic economists or business journalists. By and large, middle-class, professional people tend to start off with the image of a society basically just and agreeable, though admittedly with many faults and limitations. Industrial workers, on the other hand, tend to start off with the image of a society basically unjust, in which they have to struggle to win their just deserts from the powerful bosses.

Most Christians are middle class, and hence they often find trade union militancy, for instance, hard to understand and sympathize with, especially in an inflationary situation, though the experience of groups like teachers and nurses of falling behind their accepted comparable positions in the income scale should make such understanding easier. But there is an obvious need for those who can exercise a reconciling role, at all levels, from day-to-day conversation with friends and acquaintances, up to active involvement in collective pay negotiation and advocacy of political policies.

(*d*) *A concern for social justice*

We can sum up all these contributions in terms of an active, informed understanding and imaginative concern for social justice. Such a concern, needless to say, is not an exclusive prerogative of Christians. Many who make no Christian profession put us to shame by showing much more concern than we do. Many Christians have tended to let their concern for personal salvation blunt their interest in social justice. A healthy balance must be kept here. We believe that men's deepest needs can only be met by a personal knowledge of Christ and that we must share with others what we have found in him. But we also believe that love of our neighbour must include a concern that all men are treated justly and fairly by the institutions of society, and that they are not so warped and embittered by social injustice as to be made incapable of recognizing the love of God.

But such a concern for social justice must be thoroughgoing, rooted in actual concrete cases and prepared to go against our own interests and those of our own social group if necessary. Perhaps the greatest charge against inflation is that it involves acute social injustice. Some groups can shield themselves against it and even take advantage of it to improve their share of the national product. They include some of the better off business community who can so order their affairs as to profit from rising prices, by getting control of those types of property whose prices are most likely to rise, and can safeguard themselves against high taxation by taking advantage of all the loopholes which the tax laws allow. They also include groups of well-organized professional and manual workers who control a key skill essential to the running of the economy and can bargain for whatever rates of pay they want. Other groups have enough bargaining power, or enough political pull, to be able to ensure that their pay more or less keeps up with rising prices. But there are others who lack all such power, and they are the ones who lose out, and they tend to be among the poorer rather than the richer groups.

If such injustices are to be avoided, there must be a recognition that the legitimate pursuit of accepted self-interests by accustomed means may not be enough. Free collective bargaining, getting the best terms we can for our lads, preserving our due differentials, seeing that our pay keeps up with the onerous responsibilities of our position, all this is accepted as legitimate, yet under inflationary conditions it leads to the strong gaining from the weak, at a time when there may be little or no increase in the total size of the cake to be shared out. Similarly, the free pursuit of legitimate business activities, a sharp eye for the best profit opportunities, cutting our costs by making men redundant as soon as profit opportunities slacken off, sensibly ordering our affairs so as to avoid paying tax and thus increasing the share of the burden of maintaining those less well off which falls on others who cannot avoid it so easily; all this is good business. Yet it too results in greater injustice when inflation brings rising prices with little or no growth in the real product.

Free collective bargaining involves values which are essential both to political and social freedom and to economic efficiency, yet inflation has shown us that it cannot be regarded as an ultimate good. The community as a whole has a strong interest in the way in which relative incomes are fixed and we have to find some institutional means of ensuring this. But no such machinery can work unless the different groups are prepared to accept that their own immediate interests may have to be modified for the sake of others. Similarly, the freedom of businesses to be enterprising and efficient in making and selling what the consumers want is also of fundamental importance, but the present situation of cost inflation and poor business prospects is bringing it home to us that business freedom is not enough. The community as a whole has an urgent interest in seeing that business is both efficient and just, and we cannot rely on competition to ensure this. We have to work out the institutional forms of a partnership between business and the government which will give proper expression to this concern. This again cannot work unless all concerned, in business management, trade unions and government, are prepared to accept that their own immediate personal and group interests may have to be modified for the sake of others.

Self-interest and group interest are something to which we are all prone and we can never fully escape from it, for so much of it is unconscious. But it can be transcended if it is recognized and if we are prepared to put first loyalty to a cause which is stronger and deeper and wider than any sectional interest. This was relatively easy during the war, when there was the obvious call to co-operate and sacrifice to defend the country. It is much more difficult amid the disparate values and aims of peace time. But Christians who believe that they have a loyalty to one who himself sought not his own, but gave himself for others, should be able to give a lead, provided they have the imagination and the sympathy and the humility which such a task takes.

(*e*) *Recognition of the limits of self-interest*

Thus an essential part of our witness is the recognition of the limits of self-interest and the dangers of inordinate greed. The lesson of Christian experience is that self cannot and should not be eliminated, but that it can and must be transcended. We are to love God and to love our neighbour as ourselves. Our selfhood finds true fulfilment in loving and serving God and loving and serving our neighbour for his sake.

As we shall see later in chapter 7, an economic system based primarily on the market and the price mechanism works by channelling the powerful forces of self-interest into the service of the community, relying on the stimulus of the profit motive and the regulating force of competition. Even when there is no overall inflationary pressure, this system works with only partial success and involves much inequality and exploitation which governments have to intervene to correct. A situation of inflation puts the mechanism out of balance. The effort of each group of income receivers to safeguard or improve their position by claiming more pay, and of each group of employers to defend themselves by passing this on in higher prices leads only to a steepening spiral of prices and wages. The only ways in which market forces can bring this to an end are either through runaway inflation leading to a collapse of the monetary system, or through widespread unemployment as firms go bankrupt and discharge their workers.

In such a situation there is need for a voice which can break in and point out that the good of all demands that some shall be willing to sacrifice their short-run interests. A break in the inflationary spiral can only come if some people are willing to forego the gains which they feel they need or are entitled to, and their bargaining strength could give them. Christians should have the perspective which enables them to be clear sighted enough to see this, and the dedication which gives them the courage to say it and to back it up with appropriate action.

In times of severe inflation, Christians will often find themselves in situations where they have to decide what they are to do about pay claims or industrial action in which their work group may be involved. There will be a conflict of loyalties, for they will share the aspirations of their fellows and will want to be loyal to them, but they cannot overlook their obligations to the wider community. Our neighbours are not only our colleagues, but also those whom we serve by our work and who will suffer if we withdraw our labour, and the nation as a whole which suffers from inflation.

It is impossible to lay down any general rules which will absolve us from making our own decisions in the light of the particular situation which we find ourselves in. But we can say that those who are better off have a stronger obligation to consider the wider needs of the community than those who are worse off. When prices are rising at 20% a year, we cannot expect people who can barely make ends meet to accept a cut in their real standard of living. But we can expect those who are better off to think twice about using their bargaining power to make sure that they stay better off, and to be prepared to accept some sacrifice of their living standards if this is really going to be for the benefit of the community by making a checking of inflation possible. Unfortunately, it tends to be the better off who have the greatest bargaining power and the worse off who have the least.

Christians can thus make a vital contribution by pointing to the limitations and dangers of self-interest and excessive greed, and to the need for an altruistic motive of service to the community and willingness to make sacrifices. But it is not enough to do this merely in general principles. There must be a spelling out of what it means in particular cases, in terms, say, of a stoppage of work by teachers or doctors or bus drivers or miners, or a claim for higher pay by top civil servants or hospital consultants, or by local authority cleansing workers or hospital ancillary staff. Nor can such sacrifices be expected unless it can be clearly shown that they will not be wasted. There must be the assurance that the government, the leaders of industry and the trade unions are genuinely trying to work out and apply an effective policy to curb inflation and work towards a prosperous community in which rewards are more fairly distributed.

6. *The essential prerequisites of a workable counter-inflation policy*

We can therefore sum up fairly briefly the essential requisites for a workable policy in the present inflationary crisis.

1. First, there is no single line of policy which can be effective in a situation where demand and cost inflation are intermingled and where the general prospects are for contraction rather than expansion. There will have to be some combination of a tight general control on demand to protect the balance of payments and see that resources go into exports, with selective injections of spending power to prevent bankruptcies leading to widespread unemployment, and prevent hardship among the least well off. Along with this there must go some form of prices and incomes policy, informal if not formal, but this can only work if it is generally accepted by all concerned in industry and among trade unions and their members.

2. Secondly, there is a need for a wider and fuller understanding among the public at large of the causes and effects of inflation and of the world economic situation. In particular, there must be an understanding of how actions by any one group affect the well-being of others, whether it is groups of key workers claiming more pay, or the rich protecting themselves by speculating in commodities or by tax avoidance. Christians can play an important part here, by making themselves well informed and doing what they can to help create an alert and well informed public opinion.

3. Thirdly, no such policies can work unless there is a general belief that the government is pursuing long-term policies which make for a juster, more efficient and more compassionate society. If the next few years are to see little if any rise in the general standard of living, the community must feel that the interests of the poorest are going to be safeguarded and powerful groups are going to be restrained from getting an unfair share.

In the longer run, there must be a general belief that policies are being pursued that will make the economy more efficient and better able to meet the community's needs, both those which are best supplied by goods and services bought through the market, and those which are best supplied by the government and paid for out of taxation. A real and productive partnership between government, industrial management and the work force is essential. Britain's relationship with the rest of the world is also important, both our ability to pay our way, and our responsibilities as a rich industrial nation in a world that is still poor. The subject matter of the next four chapters is thus very relevant.

4. Finally, if such aims are to be pursued, it is essential that there should be a large and influential group of people who have a vision of the well-being of the community which transcends both the narrower interests of groups and classes, and the more blinkered dogmas of ideologies both of the left and of the right. Detailed agreement in particular policies is unlikely and probably undesirable, since the truth is too wide and our vision too limited. What is more important is a spirit that is willing to see self-interest transcended by a wider common interest, and a humility that is ready to listen to others and learn from them without abandoning deeply held principles. Christians believe that the gospel, if they are true to it, puts them in the position to provide such a vitalizing and reconciling influence. This may be the way in which perhaps above all we are called upon to commend the gospel to our neighbours in this present situation. Let us pray that we may be found ready.

Following our general plan, we now turn to the study of poverty as it is found within a rich country such as Britain. We have seen that the injustice of inflation arises largely out of the fact that it tends so often to benefit those who are already better off and to hurt especially those who are relatively poor. But why do we have a problem of widespread differences of income and opportunity in a country where most people are so much better off than they were fifty years ago? Why do we still find poverty in the midst of affluence? This is what we must consider in the next chapter.

4

Fair Shares at Home–Poverty

1. *The nature and extent of poverty in Britain today*

We begin by enquiring into the nature of poverty as it is found in Britain today. Who are the poor, how many of them are there, and what groups are most affected? But first, we must get clear on what we mean by poverty.

(*a*) *Poverty is relative*

Poverty is essentially a relative rather than an absolute phenomenon. It means falling below the standard of living enjoyed by one's contemporaries, those with whom one normally compares oneself.

In the absolute sense, poverty in Britain and the other industrialized countries of the world has undoubtedly diminished in the present century and particularly since the Second World War. The average family in Britain today is perhaps twice as well off in real terms today as it was in 1900, and even compared with the 1930s the increase is considerable. Most families are better fed, better housed, better clothed, better educated, better cared for medically and have better furniture and household goods. Most have a television set, about half of them have a car and most are able to take regular holidays away from home.

Compared with the average family in India or Africa or Latin America the contrast is, of course, even more remarkable. Yet British families are now relatively poor compared with families in the United States, Sweden or West Germany.

Even the poor today are better off absolutely than the poor of the past. In 1900 there was nothing but relief through the Poor Law for those who could not earn, and this was given on the most stringent and degrading of terms. For old people it still often meant going into the workhouse. Nowadays we have national insurance, supplementary benefits and family income supplement and in spite of their inadequacies they do in principle ensure a minimum income for all and their rates are kept in line with rises in the cost of living and in average earnings.

Yet in relative terms things are much less satisfactory. There is evidence that though average real income has risen fairly steadily at each level of the income scale, its distribution has changed very little. One recent estimate is that in both 1949–50 and 1969–70, the richest 30% of the population received a share of total income over $3\frac{1}{2}$ times as large as that received by the poorest 30%.[1] Over a much longer period of nearly ninety years, there is evidence that the earnings of the poorest 10% of male manual workers have remained remarkably constant at about 67 to 68% of average male manual earnings.[2] Although general standards of education, health services and housing have risen greatly, there is similar reason to believe that the distribution of access to these services has remained very unequal.

(*b*) *Who are the poor?*

Who are the people who suffer from poverty in Britain and how many of them are there?

The most commonly used definition is one which accepts that poverty is relative and takes as a standard the officially recognized minimum income provided by the community to those in need, namely the scale rates laid down for families of different sizes by the Supplementary Benefits Commission. To this must be added an estimate for average rent, since householder recipients of supplementary benefit normally get their rent paid in full. Using this standard, Professor A. B. Atkinson has estimated that in the mid-sixties anything between 4 and 9% of the population had incomes below this level, and this might mean between 2 and 5 million people.[3]

There are two main types of reason for individuals and families being in this position.

1. First, because of inability to earn, and because not all those unable to earn receive adequate social security.

The biggest single group of these are old people. Out of some 7·9 million recipients of national insurance retirement pensions at the end of 1973, about 1·7 million were receiving supplementary pensions to bring their incomes up to the minimum scales.[4] It is well known that there are many others who would be entitled to supplementation who do not claim it, because of ignorance of their rights, or unwillingness to accept what they feel to involve a stigma, or unwillingness to go to the trouble and inconvenience of claiming.

Other sizable groups which depend for long periods on social security include the chronic sick and disabled, the long-term unemployed, and single-parent families with young children, where the mother (or sometimes the father) is unable to go out to work. Each of these groups numbers some 200,000 to 300,000 cases.[5] Unmarried and deserted mothers are in a particularly difficult situation, since they have no national insurance benefit entitlement and are entirely dependent on supplementary benefit. All recipients of supplementary benefit are by definition living at what the community regards as a minimum level of subsistence.

In addition, some supplementary benefit receivers, who have previously been in low paid occupations and perhaps have large families, may be subject to the wage stop. If the amount of benefit to which they would be entitled under the supplementary benefit scales exceeds their average earnings when they were at work, they will not in fact be paid the amount which is supposed to represent their needs, but only the amount of their previous earnings. This is intended to prevent a disincentive to seek work, but it is bound to cause hardship.

2. Secondly, there are those who are in poverty because their earnings from full-time work are low. Sometimes this only causes poverty because they have large families, and family allowances in Britain have been too low to offset this. But recently it has become clear that there is a sizable group of working people who are poor even though they have only one or two children.

In 1973, for instance, average weekly earnings for men and for women were distributed as follows:

Distribution of average weekly earnings of weekly wage earners, 1973[6]

	Men		*Women*	
	£	% of median	£	% of median
Lowest decile	25·2	65·6	14·1	67·4
Lower quartile	30·7	79·9	16·9	80·7
Median	38·4	100·0	20·9	100·0
Upper quartile	48·1	125·3	26·7	127·6
Highest decile	60·9	158·5	34·4	164·7

In other words, among adult male wage earners, about a quarter of the total number had earnings more than 20% below the median, and about a quarter of them had earnings more than 25% above the median, leaving about half in the intermediate range. Ten per cent had earnings of less than two-thirds of the median (or £25 or less a week in 1973). Ten per cent had earnings of nearly 60% above the median (or £61 and over per week). There were thus substantial numbers both with very low and very high relative earnings. The dispersions for women workers were similar, but the actual levels much lower, with the median being only £20·9, the lower quartile £16·9 and the lowest decile £14·1. Many of the lower paid women workers are secondary earners, whose husbands are also working, but this only makes clearer the very difficult positions of many women sole earners who have to support a family.

Until recently there was no help from social security for full-time workers, apart from family allowances, which from 1968 to 1974 were at the rate of 90p per week for the second child and £1 for third and subsequent children, with no allowance for the first child. In 1971 there was introduced the family income supplement, which made a payment of half the difference between a family's actual earnings and a standard amount based on the size of the family (subject to a maximum payment). This made a good deal of difference to those who drew it, but in spite of intensive publicity, the take-up rate was poor, and it is estimated that only about half those eligible for it actually claimed it. This same limitation also applies in varying degrees to other types of means-tested benefits, such as rent rebates, rate rebates, free school meals and exemption from health service charges.

(*c*) *Unequal opportunities*

In an absolute sense once again, opportunities in Britain have expanded. Secondary education is now available to all up to sixteen, and increasingly selective schools are giving way to comprehensive schools. Opportunities for further and higher education are greatly increased, and grants are available for students, so that finance should not be a barrier. The National Health Service provides treatment as of right to everyone free or at nominal charges, so that ill-health should be a greatly reduced obstacle. Large numbers of modern houses have been built, both for letting by local authorities and for purchase by private owners. Over half the country's householders are now owner-occupiers (though in Scotland it is still only just over 30%).[7]

A closer look reveals, however, that relative inequality of opportunity has not been reduced as much as might be expected. Education is the greatest doorway to better-paid and more interesting jobs. There is, however, plenty of evidence that middle-class children, who come from homes where education is valued, and where there is a background of book culture and a value system similar to that of the schools, are able to take proportionately much greater advantage of educational opportunities than those from a manual working, and particularly from an unskilled manual working, background. Far from the disadvantages of home background being overcome, they tend to be reinforced.

One study found, for instance, that the chances of an unskilled manual worker's child being a poor reader were six times greater than those of a professional worker's child.[8] The General Household Survey found in 1973 that, whereas 38% of all school children came from the homes of white collar workers, these children accounted for 59% of all grammar school pupils and 84% of all pupils aged 11–14 in direct grant and independent schools. Of those who were still in full-time education after the age of 15, half came from non-manual backgrounds in the case of those living at home, and nearly two-thirds in the case of those living away from home.[9] Although the number of university students coming from working-class homes is much larger today than it was before the war, they still form about the same proportion of the much larger total today as they did then.

In the case of medical services, evidence as to use by different social groups is conflicting, but there is clear cut evidence that ill-health is greater among the poorer groups of the population. And it is also clear that this is true of housing, with the poorest being disproportionately concentrated into the older private rented accommodation.

In particular, the poorest groups tend to suffer from the cumulative effects of multiple deprivation, arising from low incomes, poor education, relatively poor health, bad housing conditions, a slum environment, limited job opportunities, and the resulting strains and stresses which are reflected in broken homes, juvenile delinquency and the like.

Some might argue that this represents a process of natural selection, in which those with lower innate abilities get the worse paid jobs and are less able to profit from educational and other opportunities. No doubt there is something in this, though it is almost impossible to distinguish between the effects of heredity and early environment, especially as they affect the development of children before birth and during early childhood. And in any case it could be argued that those who are disadvantaged need greater help from the social services rather than less, whereas in practice they tend to be less able to take advantage of what is provided.

2. *Why does poverty persist?*

Why has poverty in this relative sense persisted in Britain – and in most other industrial countries also – in spite of the very considerable rise in real incomes over the past thirty or forty years?

In part this is a matter of definition, inherent in the practice of measuring the extent of poverty in terms of the minimum income which the community seeks to guarantee to all its citizens. If, for instance, we take as our poverty line the Supplementary Benefits Commission's minimum scales plus average rent, and if these scales are raised periodically to keep pace with rises both in the cost of living and in average real earnings, then the proportion of the population recorded as being in poverty will automatically remain much the same, unless there has been a marked reduction in the inequality of incomes. So what we really have to look at is why there has not been such a reduction.

(*a*) *The primary distribution remains very unequal*

Most people receive their income almost entirely from work, private pensions or social security, the number having any significant amount of income from investments or property being very small. The relative levels of incomes from work reflect a mixture of the price which the market is prepared to place on the output of different kinds of services, the relative bargaining power which the providers of these services can exercise, and the institutional inertia which leads to traditional differentials between different groups of workers being preserved over long periods.

Some people are able to command a much higher price for their services than others. It may be because they have rare natural talents for which there is great demand, fostered by suitable training and experience. Examples might be pop singers, or top rank professional footballers or tennis players, or top business executives, or highly gifted mathematicians or surgeons. More importantly, opportunities to get the necessary training to make the most of such abilities are limited, both at the level of professional education and at that of opportunities for promotion once on the job.

Individual ability and opportunity probably lie behind the exceptional earnings of the fortunate few. But ability to exercise bargaining power is probably more important in explaining differentials at a rather lower level. Certain occupational groups control skills which are essential to the life and comfort of the community, and in these days of relatively full employment and effective trade union organization, they can ensure that they get what they regard as a fair reward by the threat to withdraw their services. This can apply just as much to hospital consultants or top civil servants or air-line pilots as it does to coal miners or power workers, though in varying degrees this knowledge of power is offset by a sense of responsibility towards those in the community who depend on them. Other groups are in occupations where it is much more difficult to restrict entry, or where the effects of a threat to withdraw or restrict services is much less serious. They are apt to lag behind, as the experience of teachers and many workers in local government and other public services has shown, as well as that of many less skilled workers in industry and commerce. Or they may fall behind because they are less willing to exercise bargaining power, as teachers, nurses and above all ministers of religion have been.

Conventional differentials can also persist for many years because they reflect distinctions of social status as much as of skill or bargaining power. The differentials between craftsmen and semi-skilled and unskilled workers are to some extent of this kind, though they also reflect the reward for undergoing a poorly paid apprenticeship. These differentials have been reduced in recent years, and when account is taken of earnings from bonuses, piecework and overtime, semi-skilled workers can often earn more than skilled craftsmen. But institutional and status factors are reflected, at least in part, in the differentials, in working conditions and security as much as in pay, between non-manual and manual workers, or those between doctors and nurses or physiotherapists, grade for grade. They also enter into the fact that teachers with only college of education training have lower salary scales than those with university training. They enter above all into the persistently lower pay scales for women than for men, often where the work they do shows little difference in responsibility or skill.

In so far as income is received from property or capital, the effect is to make for greater inequality, since very few people have enough property to produce a significant flow of income, apart from owner-occupied houses and rights to occupational pensions when they retire. Recent estimates suggest that somewhere between 14 and 25% of total private wealth is owned by the richest 1% of the population, and somewhere between 40 and 75% belongs to the richest 10%.[10]

It is not easy to be certain how the distribution of incomes has changed over recent decades. Over the wartime period, there was evidence of an appreciable reduction of inequality, for wartime pay increases were largely on a flat-rate basis, and thus benefited lower incomes proportionately more than higher ones.[11] Since the end of the 1940s, however, the evidence suggests that there has been little change, and that the higher income groups have managed to catch up and restore their differentials.

(b) The tax system does not do a great deal to counteract this

The system of taxation does not do as much as might be expected to counteract the inequality of the primary distribution. The British income tax is proportional over most of the range of incomes, that is to say, incomes of different levels pay the same proportion in tax, nowadays 35% of taxable income after the deduction of allowances. Since the abolition of the reduced rates, the only exceptions have been at the bottom and the top of the scales. The deduction of the flat rate personal, married and children's allowances has the effect of reducing the proportional rate of tax on the whole income, especially for larger families. At the higher levels, nowadays, above £4,500 a year of taxable income, progressively increased rates of tax are payable on successive slices of extra income, so that the marginal rate rises to 83% on all additional income above £20,000 a year. These rates undoubtedly affect the higher incomes considerably, though it must be remembered that people at this income level have more opportunities of avoiding tax through receiving expense allowances or capital gains, the latter being taxable, but at lower rates.

On the other hand, the indirect tax system, including value added tax, local rates, and the specific duties on goods like tobacco, alcoholic drinks and petrol, tends to be regressive, since it presses relatively more heavily on lower incomes than on higher ones, in so far as it is levied on the price of everyday consumer's goods and services or on houseroom. The same has been true up to the present of national insurance contributions, which have been basically flat rate, though the gradual extension of income-related contributions is making them more proportional. Overall, therefore, the tax system does little to counteract the unequal distribution of incomes, except at the very top levels.

Public expenditure, of course, does a good deal more. Social security provides incomes for those who cannot earn, such as the old, the unemployed, the sick and unsupported mothers. Services in kind like education, health and the welfare services also provide benefits to the worse off which they could not afford to buy otherwise. But part of the problem has been that the social services in Britain have not done as much in practice to redistribute income and opportunity as those who introduced the modern Welfare State hoped they would do. To the reasons for this we must now turn.

(*c*) *The limitations of the British social services*

Following the principles of the Beveridge Report of 1942,[12] British social security was developed on a basis of flat rate, uniform social insurance benefits intended to cover all the main forms of inability to earn on more or less the same terms. These were intended by Beveridge to be at a level adequate for minimum subsistence, but in fact were introduced in 1948 at rates which were too low to ensure this at what was by then regarded as an acceptable level. Although national insurance rates have been revised fairly regularly over the years and have kept up with the rises in the cost of living and in real earnings, they have never made up this initial shortfall. In October 1972, for instance, the retirement pension for a single man was only about one fifth of average weekly earnings for male manual workers, while that for a married couple was a little over a third of the same average. In particular, insurance benefit rates have been consistently below the scale rates of the National Assistance Board and its successor the Supplementary Benefits Commission, especially when account is taken of the rent allowance normally added to the latter.

It follows that retired people, the chronic sick, widows and others, if they have no other source of income, normally have to rely on means-tested supplementary benefit to bring their income up to the minimum regarded as necessary by the community. Other groups like the long-term unemployed, or single parents other than widows, have no entitlement to national insurance benefit and must rely entirely on means-tested assistance.

So far as the old are concerned, this is a situation unlike that in most Western European countries. There the aim is usually to provide everyone ultimately with an income in old age related to their average earnings before retirement, as in West Germany, France, Belgium and Sweden. Or if, as in the Netherlands, the basic pension is a flat rate one, it is fixed at a much higher level than in Britain. In no other country is there the same degree of reliance in principle on means-tested assistance, though one must add that rates and conditions of social assistance are more generous in Britain than in most of the other countries.

Some would argue that this emphasis is desirable, since it ensures that benefit goes to those who need it most and is not paid excessively to those who have other means. But the big snag is the low level of take-up of so many means-tested benefits, either because those eligible do not know that they can claim them, or because they do not want to undergo the trouble and unpleasantness of waiting about in the right offices, filling in the right forms and having their means investigated. Many retirement pensioners who would be eligible for supplementary pensions do not claim them, and low take-up is an even more serious feature of family income supplement, rent and rate rebates, free school meals and exemption from health service charges.

In the case of those who are working, the lack in Britain of a statutory minimum wage has been one factor in allowing very low rates of pay to continue, even though the minimum rates are fixed for many occupations by wages councils. Until the introduction of the family income supplement nothing was done to counteract this through social security. Low earnings at work can also lead to inability to receive full rates of supplementary benefit when not working, through the operation of the wage stop.

The social services in kind have also sometimes perversely fostered inequality of opportunity rather than counteracting it. This was true of the selective system of secondary education. Entry into grammar schools was very restricted in many areas of England (though much less so in Scotland and Wales). In some cases only 20% or so of the age group was selected. Selection was intended to be on the objective basis of ability to profit from different types of education, but in practice it was very much affected by home background, parental attitudes and quality of teaching. Moreover, those pupils who were selected for the 'superior' type of schools did consistently better over their subsequent school career and those selected for 'inferior' schools consistently worse than their previous records would suggest.

In both education and the health services the existence of subsidized fee-paying sectors within the public services also gave an advantage to the better off. They could get access to direct grant schools with low fees and high academic performance, or make use of pay beds as private patients in hospitals. Those who could afford it could, of course, also make use of facilities outside the public sector, sending their children to independent schools, or obtaining treatment privately from consultants in nursing homes. The role of these, however, raises wider issues of how far people should have the freedom to pay for what they regard as superior facilities, if they can afford them, and what effect this has on the ability of the public services effectively to meet the needs of the great bulk of the population who cannot afford an alternative.

These inequalities were perhaps most marked in the field of housing, where there has been polarization in favour of both owner-occupancy and local authority renting at the expense of the privately owned rented sector. Owner-occupiers have been subsidized by the tax allowance on mortgage interest and by the abolition of Schedule A income tax on the nominal rental of their houses, but rising prices have meant that only the better off can afford to buy their homes. Local authority tenants have also been subsidized, but by and large it is only those with steady incomes who have lived in an area for a long time who can get council houses, except where present accommodation is cleared as unfit or for redevelopment. The poorest and those least able to cope, the single parent families, the immigrants, the young couples, those rendered homeless when rented houses are improved and sold, are ones who find it difficult to get decent accommodation of any kind. Although many more people have new and well-equipped homes today than had them thirty years ago, access to them is far from even. To this we must add the effects of misguided redevelopment policies which have often resulted in tower blocks and other multi-storey buildings quickly becoming new slums in the place of old. Once again, this mainly affects those in the lower income groups, since the better off normally become owner-occupiers.

All in all, therefore, the social services in Britain have not been as effective as was hoped in preventing a situation in which, while the general level of real incomes rose, many nevertheless remained in a state of acute disadvantage.

(*d*) *The slow growth of the British economy*

Any attempts to deal with this effectively were made more difficult by the relatively slow rate of growth of the British economy, compared to other rich industrial countries. There has been no lack of pressure for improvement, particularly from those engaged in the social services. Teachers, doctors, social workers, can always see ways in which their work could be made more effective if more money could be made available. It is in the nature of the social services that the provision of one form of service, far from exhausting the demand, tends to open up new types of need. Thus if we raise the school leaving age, we must have more teachers, schools and equipment, if we start welfare work for the old or for problem families, we uncover other needs which could be met if we had more staff, and so on. There have also arisen specialist pressure groups, such as Shelter, the Child Poverty Action Group, Help the Aged and Age Concern, and there has been a growing organization among the recipients into claimants' unions, tenants' associations and the like.

But it is obviously easier to devote more resources to the social services if real national income is rising fast than if it is rising slowly or stagnant. If most people are getting better off fairly fast, tax revenue will be buoyant, and more can be spent on helping those in need without having to take more from the better off by higher tax rates. If average real incomes are rising little, if at all, more can only be diverted in this way by reducing the net real incomes of the better off. This will normally mean higher tax rates, though inflation produces the same result to some extent by carrying more people past the tax threshold and up into higher tax brackets. Higher taxes obviously produce political opposition, the more so as we cannot nowadays raise enough merely by soaking the rich, but must ask the ordinary better paid manual and white collar workers to pay higher taxes, at a time when tax rates are already high.

3. *What can be done?*

What can we do, then, to tackle the still serious prevalence of relative poverty and lack of opportunity in Britain, at a time when the country's real income is unlikely to grow fast and may even fall in the next few years?

(*a*) *How to reform social security*

The aim must be to ensure that all those who are unable to earn an income large enough to give them what the community accepts as a reasonable standard of living should receive a cash benefit adequate to guarantee it. There are various possible ways of approaching this:

1. We could fulfil the Beveridge aim of having a flat rate of national insurance benefit payable to all as of right, high enough to provide the minimum. This would mean that, for instance, all retirement pensioners would eventually be paid a standard pension equal to, say, half or two-thirds of average industrial earnings. This is the aim of the Netherlands, where the standard pension is already very near the statutory minimum wage. Similar payments would be made to the unemployed, the sick and disabled, unsupported parents and other needy groups. This would be very costly, for it involves giving more money to people many of whom

have other means such as occupational pensions. Some estimate of the extra cost can be seen from the fact that retirement pensions alone already account for well over £2,000 million annually, yet as we have seen the pension for a married couple is only about one-third of average weekly industrial earnings. It also raises other questions, such as whether unemployment insurance benefit should be unlimited in duration, as sickness benefit is, and what effects this would have on incentives to seek work.

There is also the further issue of how to provide adequate income maintenance, particularly in retirement. Those who are in better paid jobs are normally covered by some sort of superannuation or occupational pension scheme which secures them a pension related to their level of earnings during working life. The lower paid, and particularly those who change jobs frequently, are not adequately covered by such schemes. Nor can occupational schemes, which in Britain are run on the fully-funded base used by commercial insurance, easily provide protection against rises in the cost of living after retirement, still less a prospect of sharing in the national rise in average real earnings when retired.

In many other countries, and notably in West Germany and Sweden, the policy has been to provide state social insurance schemes which will eventually guarantee their participants an income in retirement equal to some percentage of their best earnings when at work, though this level will not normally be attainable until insured persons have contributed for some specified number of years, and those retiring before this have to be given some form of augmentation to bring their incomes up to a satisfactory level.

There has recently been controversy in Britain over whether this example should be followed. The Conservatives preferred a policy of encouraging occupational pension schemes and laying down minimum standards for them, and providing a State reserve scheme only on less favourable terms for those who could not be covered by occupational schemes. Labour policy was to rely mainly on a State National Superannuation system. They narrowly failed to achieve this before the 1970 election, but the Social Security Pensions Act of 1975 seems to have achieved an acceptable compromise. Under it the government will provide an earnings related pension on top of the basic one, and both will be adjusted to take account of inflation. Contributors to occupational schemes will be able to contract out of the earnings related part on relatively favourable terms, and the government will pay for the inflation proofing of their pensions. Full benefits will be achieved after twenty years of contribution.[13]

2. Alternatively, we could find ways of making payment according to needs and means more effective and avoiding the low take-up, the invidiousness and inconvenience and the heavy administrative costs associated with means tests. This would avoid making large payments as of right to those who do not need them.

The most discussed method of doing this is some form of negative income tax, using the income tax system to assess the means of those with incomes below a minimum level and make appropriate payments to them. Just as those whose incomes are above a certain level pay tax on the excess, so those whose income is below this level would receive compensation on the shortfall.

One problem with such a system is that if a straightforward payment of, say, 30% of compensation on the shortfall of income below the break-even level is adopted, parallel to the percentage tax on the excess above this point, then those with incomes below the break-even point will only receive a partial recompense, which may give them much less than they would get under our present system of national insurance and supplementary benefits. To avoid this, the break-even income would have to be fixed very high, and this would mean that many people with incomes well above the poverty line would stop paying tax and receive cash payments. We could get round this by having a hybrid system by which those with incomes below the break-even point were paid the full amount of the difference between their actual incomes and the break-even income (adjusted appropriately to take account of the number of their dependants), whereas those above the break-even point paid a percentage tax on the excess. But this would increase the amount of money needed to finance the scheme and hence the level of taxes required.

The tax credit system proposed by the Conservatives in 1972[14] was a modified form of negative income tax. It involved the replacement of the present personal, married and children's allowances against income tax, which are deductions from gross income to arrive at taxable income, by positive credits payable for the taxpayer, his spouse and dependant children. Tax would then be assessed on the whole income without deducting allowances, and the total of credits set against tax liability. If tax liability exceeded credits, the taxpayer would pay over the balance to the Inland Revenue; if credits exceeded tax liability, he would receive the balance as a cash payment. It was hoped that these cash grants could replace the present family allowances paid for second and subsequent children, as well as most payments of supplementary benefit to groups such as retirement pensioners. The proposals, have, however, aroused considerable criticism, mainly because it was not made clear where the large amount of extra revenue needed to make the payments to beneficiaries was to come from. Also the proposals as put forward involved considerable benefits through reduced tax liability to families quite a long way up the income scale.

The attraction of a system of negative income tax is its relative automaticity and administrative simplicity, but there is reason to believe that these have been overrated. The income tax machinery would have to be extended to cover many small incomes not at present assessed, and this would put a burden on the Inland Revenue Department. Moreover, any system of automatic assessment is going to be inadequate to deal with exceptional cases of need, such as high rents, or heating costs, or special attendance for the chronically sick. Some form of assistance based on test of need and means is going to be necessary to supplement any system of standardized benefits, unless these are fixed at such a generous level as to cover all conceivable needs, which would be extremely costly and wasteful.

With the return to power of the Labour Party in 1974–75, the balance therefore appeared to have swung back towards the first, or 'back to Beveridge' solution, modified only by the limited national means available.

(*b*) *How to improve the services in kind*

How can we reorganize services like education, health, welfare and housing so that they are more effective in reducing inequality of opportunity?

So far as education is concerned, it is now generally accepted that the State system of secondary schools should be comprehensive rather than selective, with pupils of all types of ability being educated in the same schools. There is controversy over how far this should be taken within schools. For instance, does streaming by ability have the same adverse effects on the less able as selection by type of school does, and should teaching therefore be in mixed ability groups? On the other hand, will this adversely penalize the more able? And are we sure that we know what kind of schooling will really enable the less academic young people to develop their potentialities to the full? Was it a mistake to raise the compulsory school leaving age to sixteen, when we were not sure that we knew what to do with the unwilling conscripts? The kind of teaching needed makes demands on teachers much greater than those involved in the traditional academic teaching of school subjects.

But two deeper questions arise. First, will not the best off always be able to secure more favourable opportunities for their children through the private sector, where they can pay for smaller classes, more highly qualified teachers and better conditions? Must we go so far as to prohibit private education if we are to prevent inequality of opportunity? Many would see equal, if opposite, dangers in such overriding of parents' freedom of choice. Secondly, can any amount of improved educational provision counteract the advantage which the child from the well-to-do, cultured home whose parents take a knowledgeable interest in his progress, will always have over those who lack these benefits?

Similar issues arise also in the fields of the health and welfare services. If inequality of opportunity is to be overcome, the emphasis must be on a comprehensive service providing appropriate treatment to all free of charge, because any imposition of charges will stop some people making use of them, even if a means test is applied. But to develop our health and welfare services to the extent where they really counteract the disadvantages which many suffer from unfavourable home background or housing would be very costly. The National Health Service is already suffering from a shortage of funds. Similar issues are raised here about the future of private provision. Many argue that the only way to get more money for the health service is to encourage those who can afford to do so to pay for themselves, yet this gives an undoubted advantage to those who can pay to bypass the queues in the public sector, and runs the risk of setting up two standards of service, a superior one in the private sector and an inferior one in the public sector.

More emphasis on prevention rather than cure, and on community care rather than hospital treatment may eventually reduce the call on national resources. These are much cheaper and if they become effective they will reduce the need for costly hospitalization. But in a situation where there is a lot of acute sickness which needs costly treatment, it is difficult to start making such a switch without even further calls on scarce resources.

The conflict is perhaps most serious in the field of housing, simply because the provision of housing costs so much. Public provision for all is an unlikely aim here, with already 50% owner-occupancy. But there is a serious problem of how to house the least well off and those who have to change houses quickly, complicated by the rapid demise of the privately rented sector.

Out of all these developments has come the concept of positive discrimination, namely that public policy should discriminate actively in favour of the most disadvantaged groups. Thus the poorest and most run down areas of our towns should have priority in the provision of new schools with more and better qualified teachers and better equipment, new health centres and hospitals, improved welfare services, and new and better planned housing. But again this is costly, and the needs of these areas must compete with urgent calls from the rest of the community for all these facilities, at a time when the country's overall real income is no longer growing.

4. *The underlying conceptual differences*

Underlying these controversies about the future course of development of the social services are fundamental differences about what their role in society should be. Ultimately, these raise questions about the nature of the society we are trying to create.

(*a*) *Minimum floor versus greater participation and equality*

Should the main purpose of the social services be a minimum one, to provide a floor below which no one should be allowed to fall, while leaving them free to rise as high above it as they can and spend their incomes as they choose? Those who hold this view will be anxious that everyone should get an adequate income for subsistence when they cannot earn through sickness, unemployment, unsupported parenthood or old age, but will feel that those who want more should provide it for themselves through occupational pensions or private insurance. They will hold that everyone should have the chance of a good basic education, access to basic medical treatment and welfare services and decent housing, but that once these are assured, it is up to them to decide what they want to spend on better educational opportunities for their children, more lavish medical treatment, or better and more congenial housing.

Others see the social services and the Welfare State in a more positive light. They see participation in them as one of the rights and privileges of citizenship, available to all. They see them as a means by which the community decides through its political organs to provide those services which it is agreed can be more effectively supplied in this way, rather than through the market. Hence the aim will not be to provide a bare minimum to keep individuals and their families out of want, ignorance, disease and squalor, but rather to provide the optimum suited to their circumstances and needs. Those who hold this view would naturally advocate income maintenance through social security benefits related to earnings. They would also support public secondary and tertiary education available without barrier of means to all who can take advantage of it, public medical and welfare services appropriate to the medical and social needs of all, and the availability of public housing to all, not merely to slum dwellers and the poorer working class.

Two other distinctions are closely bound up with this basic one. They are that between selectivism and universalism in the choice of general forms of organization, and between the market and government agencies in the choice of instruments.

(*b*) *Selectivism versus universalism*

In general, those who advocate the minimum floor concept of the social services will favour selective forms of organization. If the aim is to help those who really need to be helped, as generously as possible, it would appear to make good sense to use means tests as much as is practicable. Thus one can make sure that the help goes where it is really needed and is not wasted by being given to those who can well afford to provide for themselves. Thus one can afford to be more generous without running up an exorbitant total cost. Against this, of course, must be set the disadvantages of means tests already mentioned, in low take-up and heavy costs both to beneficiaries and in administration.

On the other hand, those who see the social services rather as the participation by the citizens in the common provision of services which are theirs by right will naturally favour a universalist form of organization. Such participation implies that cash benefits and services in kind alike must be available freely to all without test of means. Hence they must be either on a public service basis, financed entirely out of general taxation, or on a social insurance basis, with taxation disguised as insurance contributions, and minimum contribution conditions forming a socially acceptable criterion of eligibility. Against this must be set the disadvantage that such provision involves a large transfer of income in cash or kind to all who come into the prescribed categories, retired people, the sick, the unemployed, families with school children, and so on. If the provision is to be adequate to meet the needs of those who have to rely on it for subsistence, it must necessarily also give a great deal of excess benefit to the better off.

(*c*) *Market provision versus State provision*

Those who favour the minimum floor approach in general also tend to put a great deal of weight on the satisfying of wants through the market rather than through the government. They emphasize that, provided a minimum standard is guaranteed to all in need, families and individuals are likely to satisfy their wants more effectively if they are left to decide for themselves how they will spend their incomes. In particular, they should be encouraged to choose for themselves how much they want to spend on buying education, or medical treatment, or insurance to give them an income in old age, rather than on other things like clothes, steaks, television sets, cars, holidays or bingo. They emphasize also that if services like education, medical treatment and superannuation are provided through the market, competition between suppliers is likely to lead to more efficient production, with services being adapted to suit the buyers' tastes, and with a more economical use being made of labour and other resources to provide them. They tend to denounce State provision of social services as being paternalistic and argue that, provided we get the distribution of incomes right through something like negative income tax, people can be assumed to know best what they want in these fields.

On the other hand, those who favour the participation approach put more weight on the effectiveness of collective meeting of this type of want through government services. They maintain that, however important freedom of choice may be in general, the less well off families are unlikely to be in a position where they can exercise an effective choice on how much of their incomes to spend on such things as education, health services, provision for old age or similar contingencies. This is not only because those with limited means will give priority to food, light and heat and household goods, or beer, bingo and television to bring some colour into drab lives. It is also because they often lack the experience and the knowledge to enable them to choose effectively what sort of education is really best for their children, what sort of medical care they and their families need, how to insure adequately for old age, and so on. These are fields in which the educationalists and the doctors and the social welfare planners really do know better than the average citizen can do, what is in his own and his family's best interests. Nor is there much evidence that the market can provide these services more efficiently than the government can do. The economies of scale of operating a unified nationwide education, health and social security system are great enough to outweigh any diseconomies arising from bureaucracy, and a properly designed State system can incorporate a good deal of flexibility and freedom of choice.

(*d*) *How much inequality?*

Of course none of these interrelated distinctions can be pushed too far. Most people today would admit that the concept of the Welfare State implies that participation in the social services in some measure is one of the rights of citizenship, and an expression of the common concern for the well-being of fellow citizens. It is a matter of to what lengths one should push this provision and how far it should exclude private provision according to family or individual choice by those who do not want to participate in the State schemes. Similarly, most people would agree that uniform services provided as of right cannot be flexible enough to meet all types of case, and that there will always be exceptional needs that can only be met by some type of service based on investigation of the particular circumstances. It is a question of how widespread the use of means tests should be. In our mixed economy, it is generally accepted likewise that both the market and the government have important and vital roles; it is a question of where the boundary between their activities should come.

This in turn raises a more profound question to which we shall constantly be returning. How much inequality is inevitable, or indeed desirable, in our community in this imperfect world?

We have seen that inequality both of income and of opportunity is still great in Britain and in other wealthy societies, in spite of the general rise in living standards. Much of it is cumulative, for those who start disadvantaged remain disadvantaged, and only the most persistent and strong-willed among them succeed in overcoming their handicaps. Great inequality causes undoubted hardship, especially to those least able to bear it, like the old, the sick and the disabled and young children. It also causes considerable resentment and a breakdown of understanding between groups and classes. Yet how far is it inevitable that those with greater abilities, more favourable home background and better access to education, training and initial good positions, will end up much better off than those without these opportunities? How far indeed are differentials in income essential to call forth a supply of those willing to undertake special training, accept positions of greater responsibility, and take the risks of business enterprise? How far can one go in redistributing income through taxation and social services without undermining the morale of those who have traditionally enjoyed social and financial advantages? Already one hears dire complaints about the breakdown of the professions and the lack of incentives to business men. How far is this mere rationalization and special pleading, and how far does it point to a real danger? This we shall return to in chapter 7, but meanwhile Christian thinking should have light to throw on such issues.

5. *What light can the Christian understanding throw on these problems?*

It may be thought that Christianity is especially relevant to the problems of the social services and the Welfare State. Christians have always seen their vocation to be not only in individual acts of compassion and help to their neighbours, but also in the organization of charitable services through which their neighbours' needs can be more effectively and systematically met. The church has pioneered most of the social services which the state has taken over because its greater resources and authority enable it to do what a voluntary body cannot do.

There is still a big pioneering role for individual Christians and groups of Christians, along with others of goodwill, in developing voluntary services to meet needs which the statutory services cannot meet, since they are bound by established procedures and limited to their prescribed powers. Of this there are still plenty of examples. Among them the Telephone Samaritans, in their work for those threatened by suicide or despair, the Simon Community, working for the down and out, or the Marriage Guidance Councils, seeking to help those whose marriages are undergoing strain, come readily to mind, among many others.

But there is perhaps another need which is even more important at present, and that is for clear thinking about the kind of issues underlying the discussion in this chapter. This comes best from people who are deeply committed to the service of society, but yet have a perspective which makes it easier for them to strive to be objective.

Such issues include, first, the importance of a caring society which can care in a positive and constructive way; secondly, the need for a balance between the sense of belonging to a community, and scope for individual development and expression; thirdly, the question of motives to serve the community raised at the end of the last section, and fourthly, a reminder that Britain is only a small part of a wider world.

(*a*) *A caring society*

It goes without saying that Christians must witness to the importance of a caring society. Men and women are intended to grow to maturity as members of a community, in which they learn to understand one another, to relate to one another by co-operation and shared experience, and to bear one another's burdens. Our concern, therefore, must be that society develops the organizations through which such caring can be actively expressed, and in our modern world this means the professional social services, for we have got beyond the stage where it can be done adequately by individual neighbourly effort.

But the caring must be intelligent, positive and constructive. We cannot be content with the doling out of money or the perfunctory provision of services, without considering whether these are meeting the real needs of the recipients, enabling them the better to fulfil what they have it in them to be and so make their own contribution to society. Hence they must not be operated on terms which degrade the recipients, or do not treat them as responsible humans. All those concerned with the planning and operation of the social services would freely recognize this, but it is easy to forget it in the midst of the pressure of day-to-day operations and urgent short-term problems.

Such concern can be shown at several levels. Many Christians are actively engaged in the social services, as teachers, doctors, nurses, social workers or administrators. They will be trying always to see their own work in this wider perspective, as a meeting of person with person and not merely as a job by which to get a living, or a chore by which one deals with as little trouble as possible with awkward pupils, patients, clients or colleagues, or as a field in which one builds up a good reputation with those who count, so as to get promotion.

Others will express their concern by taking part in various forms of voluntary service, and will be trying to do this in the same spirit, and not merely as a cure for boredom or a means of satisfying one's own ego.

All are concerned as citizens with the wider issues of the Welfare State which we have been considering above, such as the reasons why poverty and lack of opportunity persist in the wealthy societies of today and how they can best be overcome in a mixed economy which also values individual freedom and has limited resources to spare because of its general economic difficulties.

This reminds us that if we are to care in a constructive, intelligent and responsible way, we must see the social services as part of the operation of the whole economic, political and social system. In our compassion for the old age pensioners, the low-paid workers and the delinquent ROSLA kids we will not forget the skilled craftsmen who feel that their status is being eroded by the erosion of their differentials, the young professional man struggling with a mortgage and the early stages of becoming established in his profession, or even the burdened business executive struggling to keep his business afloat against inflation, or the top civil servant taking home his load of important papers each night. These may not have the same urgent need of help, and may, we feel, be narrowly selfish in defending their threatened interests, but they too are part of the caring and to-be-cared-for community. They have their needs and their fears and anxieties. A system of social services, however technically perfect, will never succeed if it ignores the feelings of those who have to pay for it, and the effects of its operations on the rest of society.

(*b*) *Community and individuality*

The Christian also has a contribution to make to the tension between opposite concepts of the Welfare State discussed in section 4 of this chapter.

Christian theology and experience teach us that both community and individuality are essential to a healthy society. We are individuals, with unique personalities and a unique relationship with our heavenly father. We are also members of the Body of Christ and hence members one of another. This has to be worked not only within the church, but in all aspects of the life of society. Men and women, to develop fully, need to participate in a community, and this applies at all levels; to the family, the work group, the neighbourhood, but also to the nation. The social services are one of the ways in which the community expresses its concern for all members of the community, and therefore participation in them should be seen as an essential part of the expression of this concern. They are not merely a grudging dole by the comfortable to the unfortunate, not just a way by which we salve our conscience about those less well off than ourselves. We can therefore participate in them freely for ourselves and our families without feeling any stigma of 'charity' in the wrong sense of that word, but rather as an expression of that true charity described by St Paul in I Corinthians 13.

But men and women, as children of God, also need the freedom to develop and express their individuality. They need to be able to spend their money responsibly as seems good to them on behalf of themselves and their families, to provide for their children's education and future, to use their talents in building up a business or a professional reputation. A society of rigid conformity to an established ideology, where the State services take up the whole of a man's loyalty and time, and there is no space for the original and unconventional character, soon becomes stultifying and dead. Christians must recognize and respect every man's right to 'do his own thing', provided he does it in such a way as to respect and consider others.

Christians should be better placed than most to recognize and accept the inevitable tensions between these two ideals, both of which must be followed in the social services as in all aspects of life. On the one hand we believe that God has made us above all for himself, to develop to the full the individual talents and personalities which he has given us, that in his house there are many mansions suited to each of us, and that in his service there is perfect freedom. On the other hand we believe that true freedom consists in dedicating all our talents to him and in seeing all men as our neighbours who are to be loved and served for his sake, and that it is he who loses his life who shall find it. We ourselves will feel this tension, for some of us will be drawn more to the individualistic do-your-own-thing approach, and some more to the collective community-participation approach. However, because of the perspective in which we live our lives, we should be better able to see the dangers of an excessive emphasis on either side, and help to provide a corrective both in policy discussions and in practical action.

(*c*) *Incentives and inequality*

We raised in the last section the issue of how much inequality is essential to provide incentives to business enterprise and the holding of more responsible and highly-skilled posts. There is considerable evidence that, at the higher end of the scale at any rate, other incentives such as the prestige of business and professional success, or the satisfaction of doing a good job or building up a firm, the exercise of power, or the desire to serve the community, are in fact more important than merely making money. We also all know many examples of people in relatively poorly paid jobs, like many nurses, teachers or social workers, not to mention ministers of religion, who most certainly do not do their jobs primarily for the love of money. Yet money, and the social status and style of life that goes with it, has come to be the accepted symbol of success in our society, and it would be unrealistic to expect that the incentive of material reward could be dispensed with, except in an ideal Utopian order.

Christians ought to have something to say here also. We believe that the only way of life which can bring real satisfaction is one in which effort is not undertaken for material reward for oneself, whether in the form of money, prestige or power, but rather out of loyalty to a cause which transcends ourselves and a desire to serve others as part of our service of him who is the Lord of life. We have to try to witness to this truth in the way we do our own jobs and to commend it to those who are caught up in the rat race.

We must take care, however, to avoid self-deception. It is only too easy to maintain that for us service to others comes first in our jobs, while at the same time we are content to sit back and enjoy the comfortable material standard of life which it brings, and are inclined to resent others who do not have our professional training achieving a level of income as big as ours or even bigger. It is easy to feel that we are being called to new enterprises merely because they offer a wider and more responsible sphere of service, while discounting the fact that they bring us more money and prestige also. Not that this is necessarily wrong, but our motives are so often mixed. We must therefore always be prepared for the challenge to take up a job for which perhaps we are particularly well suited, which may be less well paid or less secure than the one we have, or to forego the financially attractive job if it gives us less opportunity to give of our best. Nor must we look askance at those who do the hard, dirty, monotonous jobs on which our comfort depends, if they feel that they need more money to induce them to go on doing them.

(*d*) *The wider world*

Finally, we must not forget that Britain is part of a wider world. In spite of all our present difficulties, slow growth, inflation, balance of payments problems, threatened slump, problems of poverty and lack of opportunity, we are still among the world's minority of rich nations. Average incomes in Britain are about twenty times what they are in most of Asia and Africa and, say, ten times what they are in most of Latin America. Even our poor, real though their poverty is by comparison with the rest of us, are well off compared with the drought stricken peasants of parts of India, or the Sahel region of West Africa, or with the street dwellers of Calcutta or the shanty town dwellers of Lima or Rio de Janeiro.

Here Christians have an important role to play in ensuring that we do not let our own troubles blind us to our responsibilities to those less well off. We must urge that our financial difficulties are not made the excuse for cutting down on overseas aid, though of course we must also make sure that it is used effectively. Nor must we allow our inflation and balance of payments difficulties to be made the excuse for trying to beat down the price of agricultural raw materials, which come to us from poor cocoa growers in Ghana, or poorly-paid tea plantation workers in Ceylon, or sugar plantation workers in the West Indies. Nor must we let these difficulties be used to justify closing our markets to the cheap cotton goods and other manufactures which countries in the Third World can sell to us, because of their abundant cheap labour.

Thus the question of fair shares must be looked at internationally as well as nationally. This involves investigation of the reasons for the acute division of the world into rich and poor countries today, and the prospects for the poor countries breaking out of the poverty in which they are entrapped. This we take up in the next chapter.

5

Fair Shares Internationally–World Poverty and Development

1. *The problem of world poverty*

We live in a world of sharp contrasts between rich and poor. About a third of the world's people, in North America, Western Europe, Australia and New Zealand and Japan, live in countries which can be called rich. Although there is much relative poverty among them, yet the bulk of the people have a standard of living such as in all past ages has only been the privilege of a wealthy minority. There are a few countries in an intermediate position, with still a large number of people poor and under-privileged, especially in the rural areas, but with a steady progress towards rising incomes among the more urbanized population. Among them one might include Southern and Eastern Europe, and more doubtfully Mexico, Argentina, Chile and Brazil, and perhaps South Africa, though here there are sharp contrasts between white and non-white. For the rest, the great bulk of the people of Asia, Africa and Latin America, the picture is one of the masses being sunk in poverty, as subsistence peasants or landless labourers, and only a tiny minority of professional, commercial and industrial workers and of landowners having standards of living comparable to those of the rich countries.

(*a*) *Rich and poor in one world*

Statistical evidence of differences in standards of living is always subject to difficulty. Many countries have poor and unreliable statistics, and in any case one is comparing urbanized, industrial, market economies with mainly rural, subsistence economies, in which most people handle little money and provide for themselves most of the services which we in the West have to buy and pay for. Nevertheless, some figures from

Social Indicators in Rich and Poor Countries[1]

	Average income: £ per head	School enrolments (% of age group): 1st level	2nd level	Infant mortality: rate per 1,000 births	Life expectancy: years at birth	Food consumption per head: Protein grammes	Calories
Poor countries							
Botswana	40	(7–13) 78	(14–18) 7	—	43·5	—	—
Chile	212	(7–14) 106	(15–18) 34	91·6	63·6	65·4	2,516
Ghana	80	(6–15) 56	(16–21) 54	87·5	48·5	43·5	2,084
India	48	(6–12) 56	(13–17) 15	—	51·8	50·6	1,964
Indonesia	40	(7–12) 72	(13–18) 11	—	48·1	38·4	1,760
Kenya	60	(6–12) 60	(13–18) 8	—	50·0	67·9	2,243
Egypt	72	(6–11) 70	(12–17) 31	118·0	52·9	76·6	2,639
West Malaysia	149	(6–11) 89	(12–18) 35	42·2	60·7	49·4	2,200

	Average income: £ per head	School enrolments (% of age group): 1st level	2nd level	Infant mortality: rate per 1,000 births	Life expectancy: years at birth	Food consumption per head: Protein grammes	Calories
Rich countries							
Irish Republic	517	(4–11) 104	(12–16) 52	19·2	73·0	91·5	3,455
England and Wales	851	(5–10) 106	(11–17) 71	18·6	72·4	88·6	3,233
Scotland		(5–11) 98	(12–19) 50				
France	1,160	(6–10) 120	(11–17) 70	15·1	73·5	98·2	3,108
Israel	696	(6–13) 94	(14–17) 56	23·6	73·1	86·6	2,827
Sweden	1,622	(7–12) 96	(13–18) 100	13·1	75·3	80·4	2,907
United States	1,894	(6–12) 110	(13–17) 101	19·8	70·6	93·7	3,156

Poverty Report 1974, edited by Michael Young, can be used to throw light on the contrast.

The two groups are not, of course, uniform throughout. For instance, among the poor group, average income per head varied from £40 in Botswana and Indonesia up to £149 in West Malaysia and £212 in Chile. Among the rich group it varied from £517 in Ireland and £696 in Israel up to £1,622 in Sweden and £1,894 in the United States. There were similar variations in the other indicators, though in the case of school enrolments, these reflect to some extent differences in the age range covered. For instance, the comparatively low secondary education coverage of 50% shown for Scotland is mainly the result of the age range covered being 12–19 (as against 11–17 in England and Wales), with inevitably lower enrolments among the 17 and 18 year-olds. Similarly, the enrolments of over 100% shown for some countries reflect the fact that the schools concerned contain some pupils outside the specified age range.

Nevertheless, the differences between rich and poor countries shown up in these examples are highly significant. The poor countries have average incomes per head ranging from a tenth down to a twentieth or less of those in the rich countries. While their coverage of children in primary schools is sometimes quite respectable, in secondary schools coverage is still very low. Infant mortality is much higher, life expectancy at birth is considerably lower, and nutritional standards are also lower.

(*b*) *The characteristics of underdeveloped countries*

The developing countries, as it is now polite to call them, obviously vary enormously.

Some, like China, India, Pakistan, Indonesia or Brazil, are vast in area and have very large populations, ranging upwards from Brazil's 90 million to India's or China's 600 million. Some, like many of the African states, though large in area compared with European countries, have very small and scattered populations of only a few millions. Others again are very small in area, like Singapore, Mauritius and the Caribbean Islands, but may have very dense populations.

Some of the larger countries, though the majority of their people are still very poor and mostly rural, yet have well-developed industrial, commercial and financial sectors and a large force of well-educated and trained intellectuals. This is true, for instance, of China, India, Mexico, Brazil and Egypt. Others, like some of the African countries such as Niger, Chad, the Central African Republic or Upper Volta, may have little or no industry or large scale commerce, few educated experts and almost all their people still in a state of tribal agriculture.

Some countries have great natural resources, actual or potential, such as rich agricultural land, large mineral reserves and plenty of unexploited hydro-electric power. Much of Latin America comes into this category, and so do African countries like Nigeria, Kenya, Zaïre and Tanzania, or Asian countries like Burma, or Thailand, or Iran. Some of the Arab oil producers like Saudi Arabia, Kuwait and the Gulf States are extreme examples of this. Populations are small and oil revenues so high that some of them have incomes per head among the highest in the world, yet these countries are largely desert with few other resources.

At the other extreme one might put countries like Argentina, Uruguay and Chile. In the past these developed relatively high incomes through selling meat or grain or minerals on the world market, but unlike Australia or Canada or New Zealand with similar economic bases, they failed for various social and political reasons to make the breakthrough into sustained growth and full development.

Nevertheless, in spite of this diversity, it is possible to point to certain general characteristics which all the developing countries share in varying degrees, and out of which their difficult problems of development mainly arise.

1. Not only are they poor, but they are also characterized by extreme inequality of incomes. The great bulk of the population will commonly be peasants or tribesmen, scratching a bare living from tilling the soil or rearing animals, or else unskilled labourers, chronically under-employed, or petty traders, or beggars. But in most countries there is a tiny minority of rich landowners, merchants and industrialists who have incomes as high as any in the West, and much less eroded by taxation. There is also usually a rather larger group of workers in the public services and employees in modern industry and commerce, who, though their pay is commonly low by Western standards, rank as rich by comparison with most of their compatriots.

2. This inequality arises out of the fact that the economies of these countries tend to be overwhelmingly agricultural. Frequently 70, 80 or even 90% of the population will live in the rural areas and will be more or less dependent on agriculture, though their low productivity means that agriculture accounts for a smaller proportion of the national product than it does of the labour force. Service occupations will commonly account for up to 20% or so, largely taken up with petty trading and

personal service, but manufacturing may occupy 10% or less, and that will include handicrafts.

3. It follows that political power is commonly in the hands of the landowners, allied with whatever wealthy groups of traders and industrialists which may exist. This tends to be true irrespective of the nominal constitutional position, whether it is a parliamentary democracy, a monarchy or some sort of dictatorship. The bulk of the people are too poor and too ignorant to be able to exercise effective political power. Elections can be rigged and legislatures and executives filled with the supporters of the ruling groups. The chief modifying factor is apt to be the role of the army, which, being one of the few groups with technical training, equipment and discipline, tend to think of themselves as the embodiment of the nation as against sectional interests, and hence to interfere decisively in politics from time to time.

4. Foreign trade tends to be both limited and specialized. In relation to the national product, it is usually relatively unimportant, since most of the people are largely self-sufficient and have not got the means to be large importers. Exports, however, tend to be highly specialized on one or two goods, usually either minerals or basic agricultural products. Thus Ghana is dominated by cocoa, Brazil and Colombia by coffee, Ceylon by tea, the Central American states by bananas, Mauritius and the Caribbean islands by sugar, Zambia by copper, Malaysia by tin and rubber, Bolivia by tin. They are thus very vulnerable to fluctuations in the world supply of and demand for their staple export products, which produce severe fluctuations in prices and hence in export earnings.

5. The trade in these staple products is usually dominated by expatriate firms from the West. In many cases European and American companies have established the mines and the plantations, and also handle the export of the goods, while the necessary technical, managerial and financial expertise also comes from abroad. In other cases, like Ghana's cocoa and Nigeria's palm oil, the actual production is in the hands of peasant farmers, but the financing and exporting is still in expatriate hands. Thus there arises the phenomenon of the dual economy, with a foreign-based modern sector existing side by side with a traditional indigenous sector, but with little effective interplay between them.

6. This brings us back to the acute shortage in most such countries of all the infrastructure needed for development. Most of the people are probably illiterate, or will have only a few years of low quality schooling. There is a lack of people with all kinds of technical, technological,

administrative and clerical skills. The general level of health and nutrition is usually poor, and medical services very limited, especially in rural areas. Water supplies are often poor, sanitation non-existent, electricity supply very limited, roads, railways and ports seriously inadequate. The means are just not present to allow the bulk of the people to take part in a growing and developing economy.

7. On top of this comes the one decisive change which contact with the rich world has brought, namely the rapid fall in mortality and the consequent population explosion. Modern medicine has resulted in the checking of many of the killer diseases, like malaria, cholera, yellow fever, typhus and so on, and the alleviation of many others. Many children and young people who used to be carried off now grow to maturity and themselves start families. Crude death rates have commonly fallen from 25–30 per thousand or more to 15 per thousand or less. Fertility, on the other hand, has not been checked, in spite of family limitation campaigns. For the poor peasant, the best insurance against old age still seems to be a large family, even though nowadays all five or six of them may grow up, instead of perhaps one or two as in the past. The average age of the population is low. Frequently half will be aged twenty or less, so that the large number of new families being started will mean that rapid population growth will continue for some time even if family size falls. Thus these countries are commonly faced with a population rising at some 2 to 3% a year. Hence they must provide food and maintenance for a substantial number of extra people each year before there is any margin for raising living standards.

2. *A widening gap?*

Of course, a situation in which the bulk of the people are in dire poverty and only a small number are comfortably off or wealthy is nothing new. Indeed, it was the normal state of most of the world, from the time when settled agriculture and urban life began in Egypt and Mesopotamia around 4000 BC, up to a century ago. The new and exceptional position is the rise to affluence of the industrial countries of today. How did this come about, and why does not the rest of the world follow suit?

(*a*) *The breakthrough to sustained growth*

Historical circumstances in Western Europe in the late eighteenth century, and especially in Great Britain, were uniquely favourable to the advent of what came to be called the Industrial Revolution. For several centuries back national governments had been developing, efficient enough to guarantee law and order, and enlightened enough to encourage industrial and commercial enterprise. Merchants were developing organized trade both at home and abroad, building up financial institutions to sustain it, and accumulating capital to invest in its extension. There was a considerable growth of manufactures, both handicrafts as in textiles and on a large scale, as in iron working, glass making, dyeing, brewing and similar trades. This provided products which trading countries like the Netherlands, Britain and France could export to the rest of the world. Agricultural improvements meantime ensured an adequate food supply. Out of this situation arose the decisive breakthrough of the application of technology to manufacturing and transport, which enormously increased productivity by economizing on human effort. The steam engine was applied, first to cotton spinning and weaving, then to water and land transport, and later to all industry. There were improvements in the technique of ironworking, such as the use of coke for smelting and the puddling process for making wrought iron, which were the beginnings of modern metallurgy and led on to large-scale engineering and steel making. There were similar revolutionary developments in chemical manufacture.

Once these developments began, they expanded cumulatively, as business firms ploughed back their profits into further investment and innovation. Britain had a head start in industrialization, but after the end of the Napoleonic Wars the process spread through trade and investment into the countries of Western Europe with similar historical and social backgrounds, like Belgium and France, and also into the United States with its immense natural resources. In the mid-nineteenth century it spread into Germany, Austria, Italy and Scandinavia, and later still into Russia and Japan, and into the more recent countries of overseas European settlement, like Canada, Australia and New Zealand.

The enormous advantages in productivity which the industrial nations developed, through steam and later electric power and internal combustion, and through the growing application of technical knowledge to the processes of production and transport, put them in a very favourable position relative to the rest of the world. With their capital and technical know-how, and with the development of steamships and railways, firms in Europe and North America could invest in developing the agricultural and mineral resources of Asia, Africa and Latin America, as well as those of their own homelands. By the late nineteenth century they were assured of cheap supplies of foodstuffs and raw materials. With their superior productivity they could undercut native craftsmen and sell cheap manufactured goods to the rest of the world in exchange for their primary products.

With economic power went political power, so that the West came to control most of the rest of the world, either directly through colonial empires, as in most of Africa and Asia, or indirectly through influence over independent governments, as in China or Latin America. In either case, the industrial and commercial interests of the West were able to strengthen their already very strong position in the Third World and make sure that they continued to get access to their markets on favourable terms.

(*b*) *Why did this process not spread?*

Why has the process of successive take-off into sustained growth not spread beyond those countries where it was already effectively under way by about 1914? Why in particular, with the exception of Japan, has it not spread outside the countries of Europe or of European settlement?

In some cases, as in most of Africa, the gap in culture and technology was just too great for fruitful contact. There were some exceptions, for instance in West Africa, where climate and disease long barred effective residence by Europeans, there was a partnership in trade between British merchants and African merchants in the coast towns, and a development of a considerable African bourgeoisie. But the tribal social structure and the low level of technology, together with the damage done to fruitful co-operation by the slave trade, meant that the shock effect of European penetration was usually too great for constructive African response. Initiative and control remained firmly in European hands. The same was basically true of much of rural Latin America, where small elites of former Spanish and Portuguese colonists exercised a feudal domination over still largely unassimilated Amerindian tribesmen and peasants.

But what about countries with great historic cultures and thriving technologies, like China, India, parts of South-East Asia and the Middle East? Why did they not respond, whereas Russia and Japan did? The reasons are not clear, and probably vary in each case. Social factors are sometimes the clue, a feudal structure too rigid to give scope for commercial and industrial enterprise, power concentrated in the hands of landowners with no interest in change. Sometimes arbitrary and despotic government did not allow enough security from exploitation or disorder to make enterprise attractive. Ideological factors also came in, for instance the lack of interest in material progress induced by some aspects of Hindu and Buddhist belief, or the caste structure associated with Hinduism, or the fatalism often characteristic of Islam.

Colonial control has undoubtedly been a factor in many cases, for colonial governments tended to operate primarily for the benefit of industry and trade in the Mother Country. Thus the Government of India long kept the Indian market freely open to British exports, so that the highly developed local cotton handicraft industry was largely wiped out by competition from cheap Lancashire cotton goods, and the establishment of a mechanized Indian cotton industry was delayed. Later, with the rise of Indian political power and the beginnings of partial self-government, tariffs were introduced to protect Indian industries. On the other hand, in China, it was political unrest and the weakness of the central government which hampered industrial development, as is shown by the rapid rise of factories in Shanghai and Hong Kong under foreign protection.

Most parts of the Third World thus came to exhibit the characteristics of the dual economy. There was an expatriate sector, based on foreign capital and enterprise, developing mineral and agricultural resources for export to the industrial countries, and frequently dominating foreign trade. It was manned largely by expatriate experts, it commonly provided its own infrastructure of banks, merchant houses, transport and power facilities and the like, and most of its profits were remitted back to the homeland. There was an indigenous sector of subsistence agriculture, domestic food supply and handicrafts, and in some cases a modest amount of factory industry serving mainly the home market. There were some exceptions, for instance by the 1930s India and Hong Kong were large exporters of cotton goods, but by and large the foreign-based modern sector did little to spark off development in the indigenous sector. The mines and plantations trained a certain number of technicians and administrators and provided a large part of the export earnings, as well as an important tax base. A few well-off groups in the cities became large importers of manufactured goods from the West to meet their higher consumption standards. But the traditional life of the villages continued almost unchanged.

With the attainment of political independence in the 1950s and 1960s went a strong desire to break out of this situation of economic dependence, but there are many obstacles in the way of doing so. Not only have the developing countries faced all the problems of 'backwardness' summarized in the first section of this chapter, but they have frequently found that the balance of world economic power is weighted against them. They are dependent on the industrial countries for specialized plant and equipment of all kinds and for the technical expertise necessary to use it. Frequently these must come from particular large firms which have developed the plant and the skills necessary. They also find that the same business interests in the same countries control the markets in which their products are to be sold, the shipping and other transport facilities needed to carry them, the banking and insurance services needed to finance them. It is often alleged that the overt political colonialism of the past has only been replaced by a neo-colonialism exercised by large American and European firms.

This situation is not primarily the result of deliberate exploitation by the big international companies. Rather, it is because their greater experience, skill and resources put them in a dominant position. Their primary aim is to make profits for their shareholders and to increase the scale of their operations, and while not unmindful nowadays of their impact on less developed communities, they are apt to put commercial considerations first. Nevertheless cases have not been wanting, especially in the relationships between the United States and Latin America, where large American companies have been able to induce the American government to intervene on their behalf against moves by local government which go against their interests.

It was frequently claimed in the 1950s and the 1960s that the terms of trade were moving inevitably against the primary producing countries. As output and incomes rose in the industrial countries, the demand for basic foodstuffs and raw materials did not rise proportionately, it was argued. There was greater economy in their use, so as to get more output of finished goods out of a given input of primary materials. There was a switch to less raw-material-intensive forms of production, e.g. from cotton textiles to electronics, and growing use of synthetics like artificial rubber, plastics and nylon. People do not increase their food comsumption as their income rises, and they switch to more highly processed foods with less raw material content in their value. Thus the world price of primary products would tend to fall.

At the same time inflation in the industrial countries was pushing up the prices of their exports of manufactured goods, which the developing countries needed to buy. Thus the latter, still largely dependent on primary product exports, found the prices of their imports rising while those of their exports were falling, and thus found it increasingly difficult to earn enough foreign exchange to pay their way and meet their need for imports of machinery, fertilizers and so on required for development.

This type of trend did take place in the late 1950s and early 1960s, but the fall in primary product prices was largely a reaction from their earlier rise during the Second World War and the even steeper post-war rise to a peak in 1951 at the time of the outbreak of the Korean War. In the later 1960s they began to rise again and their very steep rise in 1973–74 makes it clear that there is no inevitable downward trend. At that time the pundits began to talk again, as they had in the late 1940s, about an equally inevitable long-term trend towards a relative rise in primary product prices, as spreading industrialization leads to a growing world demand, especially for key metals and fuels, and as cheaper resources begin to get worked out. More must be said about the whole question of resources, supplies and prices in the next chapter. What is true is that these prices are very unstable and liable to fluctuate violently. Already by early 1975 they had fallen by about a fifth from the peak level of a year earlier.[2]

In spite of all these difficulties, has the gap between the rich and the poor countries been growing? In terms of absolute growth of output, the developing countries as a whole have not done badly. In the 1950s and 1960s they achieved an overall rate of growth of real output of about 5% annually, about the same as the developed countries taken together. A number of qualifications must, however, be made.

1. First, this 5% overall figure conceals very different achievements by different countries. Some, like Malaysia, Mexico, Brazil, Taiwan or South Korea grew very fast indeed; others, like India, with larger populations and less unused natural resources, were much less successful, while others, like some of the very backward countries of Central Africa, found it difficult to grow at all. Others again, like Argentina and Uruguay, which were already well developed, suffered from internal political problems which led to stagnation.

2. Secondly, most developing countries had much faster population growth than the developed countries had, which meant that a large part of the increased output was swallowed up by supporting more people, and income per head rose more slowly, averaging only about 2–2½% a year.

3. Thirdly, the benefits of growth were by no means evenly spread among the people. Much of the increase of income went to the rich

farmers and landlords who could make use of the agricultural innovations associated with the so-called 'Green Revolution'. They could grow the new and much more productive strains of wheat, maize or rice, which needed irrigation and artificial fertilizers and expert handling, which the poor peasants could not afford. Or else it went to the industrialists and merchants of the cities who developed consumer goods industries serving a small market of the well-to-do, and to the relatively highly paid factory and office workers whom they employed. The smaller peasants, the landless labourers in the countryside, and the masses of unskilled workers who flocked to the towns, gained little benefit.

4. Fourthly, the figures of the growth of real output in total or per head are only a very poor measure of how living standards are being improved, especially when we are comparing countries with very different patterns of life. Statistics of output and even of population are very poor and doubtfully accurate in many countries. In particular, it is very difficult to measure accurately that large part of output which consists of food grown for themselves by peasant families, or handicraft goods made for themselves, or houses built for themselves. But if these people move to the town they have to buy many of these things. Nor, of course, can any measure be made of the quality of life enjoyed by a peasant or tribal community with simple tastes and a rich community culture, as compared with the same people when they have moved to become shanty slum dwellers in the city.

5. Fifthly, the initial differences in material living standards between the rich and the poor countries were so great that talk about increasing or reducing gaps can be very misleading. If one country starts off with an average income of £1,000 per head and another with £50, even if both grow at 5% a year the gap between them will increase. In the first year, for instance, it will be £950, but in the following year it will be £997·50 (i.e. £1,050–£52·50). After ten years it will be £1,512·40, i.e. £1,592–£79·60. Dr A. P. Thirlwall has estimated that even for those developing countries whose income per head is growing faster than that in the developed world, the prospects for 'catching up' are gloomy. For instance, at the growth rate of the 1960s it would take Western Malaysia 494 years to catch up with the United States, and Pakistan 1,760 years, while to reach income levels per head equivalent to those of Western Europe or the United States by the year 2000, most developing countries would have had to have a rate of growth of output per head of 8 to 10% a year.[3]

In these circumstances, the concept of 'catching up' or 'closing the gap' makes little sense. Indeed, it is doubtful whether it would be appropriate or desirable, even if possible, for the developing countries to aspire to follow the same pattern of industrialization and urbanization which both the West and the Soviet Union have followed. They have already had all too much experience of rapidly growing urban slums, like those of Europe or North America in the nineteenth century, but without the fast growing employment opportunities which made London or Glasgow, New York or Chicago a tolerable escape from rural destitution. What their people aspire to is some hope of breaking out of the round of precarious subsistence, dependent on the vagaries of droughts and floods, subject to extortion by rapacious landlords and moneylenders, some chance of education and better health and nutrition. They want a rise in living standards, but one achieved in their own way, keeping their traditions and culture. Quite apart from the question whether the world's resources are adequate to enable all its people to achieve a material standard of living comparable to that of the United States today, there is reason to believe that a less urbanized, more dispersed form of development, based on smaller scale and less capital-intensive technology, is much more likely to be appropriate to their means and needs.

3. *The prospects for a breakthrough into sustained growth*

What are the prospects for the developing world of achieving a breakthrough into sustained growth? What obstacles do they face and what are the prospects of these being overcome? What effective help can be given to them by the rich countries? These issues are all interrelated and hence they are best discussed together under their various aspects, such as capital supply and aid, world trading patterns, foreign private investment techniques and know-how, and political and social factors.

(*a*) *Capital supply and aid*

When attention was first given to problems of world development in the 1950s, the emphasis was on capital supply. Development needed large-scale investment to improve the productivity of agriculture, to build up manufacturing industries and to provide the infrastructure of transport and power facilities, schools, hospitals, water supplies and so on. Poor countries with the bulk of their populations at subsistence level lacked capital. Most of the people had no margin of savings, and the rich people who had, tended to put their savings into luxury houses and flats, or to invest them abroad. Governments could raise some capital through taxation, but there were political obstacles to this, since the wealthy controlled the political system and the poor could pay but little in taxes.

There was thus a gap between the amount of saving that could be raised and the amount of investment needed, and hence a call for aid from abroad to fill this gap with grants and loans. Although those who knew the countries well stressed the social, political and institutional obstacles to rapid development, there was a certain tendency to over-simplification. Put in the capital and the growth would follow. There was a great deal of talk about capital-output ratios – i.e. £4 million of extra investment would produce an increment of output of, say £1 million (or whatever the ratio was taken to be).

From the late fifties onward an extensive international aid programme got going, and was given a further impetus by the designation by the United Nations of the 1960s as the first International Development Decade. By the early sixties there was a total annual flow of capital from rich to poor countries of some $8 billion a year, and this expanded over the decade, though it did not keep pace either with rising prices, or with the rising real incomes of the rich countries. At the end of the decade it was around $13 billion a year from the non-communist countries, plus a smaller and more variable amount from the communist countries. However, this figure included commercial investment as well as inter-governmental aid, and although commercial investment has important developmental effects, if properly used, it is misleading to consider it as aid. The total flow of funds was about 0·8% annually of the gross national products of the donor countries, but official aid amounted to only about half of this. The world financial crisis of the early seventies made it unlikely that the Pearson Commission's target figures for 1975 would be reached, of 1% of gross national product in total, to include 0·7% in official aid.[4] Moreover, there had arisen grave doubts about both the form and effects of the aid programmes.

Why did the aid programme fail to fulfil the hopes of its proponents?

1. First, because a large-scale programme of unrequited transfer of resources from one country to another was something unprecedented in history, there were considerable problems in obtaining political support for it in the donor countries. It is well known that there are no votes in aid, for the direct beneficiaries are outside the country. Therefore there was a strong tendency for politicians both to conceive of it and present it

in terms which stressed the indirect benefits which would come to the donor country. This was particularly true in the United States which because of its size and wealth and predominant role in the Western world was called upon to contribute the largest total amount of aid, though not the biggest proportion of its national product. The separation of powers in the American constitution means that American administrations face peculiar difficulties in persuading the two houses of Congress to accept and support their spending proposals. Similar, though more discreet influences were not lacking in other countries like Britain and France.

The danger was that disillusionment set in when the expected benefits were not achieved. For instance, in the United States the aid programme was sold largely as a means of obtaining support for American policies in the days of the Cold War, and there was inevitable disappointment when many of the recipient countries took political lines which were regarded as unduly favourable to Russia or China, or when they interfered with the activities of American companies in their territories. Thus the United States for long tended to favour Pakistan rather than India because of the latter's neutralist position and alleged friendliness to Russia. Another result was that a disproportionate amount of aid went to countries with regimes regarded as anti-Communist and favourable to the United States, even if they are also dictatorial and often corrupt and inefficient as well. Examples include South Vietnam, South Korea, Taiwan, the Philippines and Thailand, as well as some of the less attractive dictatorships in Latin America.

British aid similarly has gone in large measure to former colonial territories in Africa, but when Tanzania broke diplomatic relations with Britain in 1966 over Rhodesia, aid was cut off, though many would feel that President Nyerere's brand of African socialism provides probably the most hopeful policy of achieving a viable form of development of any country in the Continent. The French have achieved about the highest level of non-military aid in relation to their national product, but it has mostly gone to their former African territories, where they have spent very generously in financing the salaries of French teachers and administrators, in the hope of maintaining French political and cultural influence. But when Guinea refused to remain associated with France in 1958, aid was immediately cut off.

The danger is that if the electorate is persuaded to support aid on the grounds that this will bring short term political benefits, the disillusionment when these hopes are disappointed may lead to an equally strong reaction. This has certainly happened in the United States, where Congress has severely cut the aid programmes in recent years.

2. Similar considerations have affected the forms which aid has taken. Because the donor countries have wanted to make certain that their taxpayers' money is spent effectively, they have insisted on most of their aid being bilateral, that is direct from donor to recipient, rather than multilateral, through United Nations agencies. They have also tended to apply it to specific and identifiable projects, such as dams and irrigation schemes, or power stations, or harbour developments, or hospitals, rather than allowing it to be used to support general development programmes, for instance to pay for essential raw materials or spare parts for established industrial plant.

They have also sought to tie a large part of their aid to being spent on goods exported from their own countries, or salaries for experts drawn from among their own citizens or, as the Americans have done, insisted on a large proportion of the goods being carried in their own ships. Although aid tying has sometimes meant that more aid was made available than if there had been no such strings, it has also reduced its value to the recipients, since they have had to spend it on goods and services which are often more expensive and less suitable.

A considerable proportion of aid has also taken the form of loans, often at rates of interest not much short of commercial rates, rather than grants or interest-free loans. This has led to a serious burden of debt interest and repayment on the recipients, which often swallows up a large part of each year's aid receipts. The Pearson Commission found that, in the mid-sixties, and taking public and private loans together, debt service took up 87% of new loan disbursements to Latin America and 73% to Africa, though only 40% to South Asia and the Middle East.[5]

The result has been that aid has not been as valuable to the recipients as it might have been, and that there has been constant friction between the plans and priorities for development, as drawn up by the governments of the developing countries, and the donor governments' ideas about what policies should be followed. Admittedly, many of the governments in the developing countries have been weak and inexperienced, short of able administrators, unstable and sometimes corrupt. Admittedly, sometimes the donor countries must withdraw support from regimes which they believe to be so misguided or tyrannical as to be unable to secure the best interests of their people. But by and large, it must be assumed that the leaders of the countries concerned know better what suits their country and is practicable than the leaders of a European or North American government can do.

3. At the same time, it is true that wrong emphases in both recipient and donor countries have tended to cause development investment to take forms not always appropriate to the countries' true needs. The temptation to go for the spectacular, large-scale project which will be a visible memorial to the politicians concerned, has been strong among the planners of developing countries as well as among donor governments. Hence we have had large-scale multi-purpose irrigation and electric power schemes where sometimes small-scale wells and dams might be more appropriate, or massive steel mills and motor plant in countries lacking the market to support them, or national airlines with spectacular airports, or multi-million pound hospitals in the capital city, or lavishly equipped universities. In many cases smaller scale technology, such as the encouragement of rural industries, or a network of village clinics, or the training of technicians, might be more effective.

In other words, capital in itself is not enough. It must be of the appropriate kind that can be used along with the resources of labour and skills available in the country.

(*b*) *World trading problems*

It was early realized that there was not only a capital gap, but also a foreign exchange gap. The developing countries needed to import plant and machinery, fertilizers, tools, raw materials and spare parts if they were to expand their production. They also needed to employ experts of all kinds from the rich countries, who would want to remit their savings to their homes. As incomes rose, their own people would also want to consume manufactured goods of all kinds which they could not produce for themselves. There was thus likely to be a gap in their balance of payments which could not easily be filled by an expansion of their exports. Aid was thus seen as a temporary means of bridging this gap, though it could not be a permanent solution unless it led to a growth of the country's exporting capacity. Moreover, in so far as it took the form of loans, it brought with it a further balance of payments burden in the form of interest and repayment obligations. Hence there has been a growing emphasis on 'trade, not aid' as the longer term solution.

Part of the problem has been the instability of primary product prices. As we saw above, the downward movement in these in the late fifties and early sixties seems to have been a temporary swing rather than a permanent trend. But instability can cause great problems to the planners of development, since countries cannot know what their export earnings are going to be and hence find it difficult to plan their imports. If export prices fall, they cannot pay for the volume of imports which they had planned for, while if they rise, the windfall gains are likely to lead to an import spree on luxuries by those who benefit, unless controls are very efficient. There have thus been many calls for international stabilization schemes for basic primary products. These are difficult to set up, since to make them workable all the main producer and consumer countries must be included, and it is difficult to get agreement between them. They are always liable to break down, for if there is a glut of the product some producers are tempted to undercut the fixed price in the hope of selling more, whereas if there is a shortage, some consumers will overbid the price in the hope of getting scarce supplies. Moreover, the agreements tend to encourage production in other countries which are not party to them, until a glut is built up which breaks down the agreed prices. At the same time, the protection of the minimum price may discourage diversification of producers into other products and markets for which prospects may be better, and thus preserve a relatively uneconomic use of resources.

But the developing countries have also suffered from the fact that the rules of international trade tend to be set by the biggest trading countries with their own interests primarily in mind. Thus the Most Favoured Nation principle embodied in the General Agreement on Tariffs and Trade (GATT) stipulates that in general no country shall give preferential tariffs or other favourable terms to one country without extending these to all other countries, with the only recognized exceptions being for complete customs unions and free trade areas like the European Economic Community. This means, for instance, that developing countries cannot help their neighbours to build up their industries by admitting imports from them at a lower rate of duty than that on the same goods from Europe or the United States, unless they are prepared to go the whole hog and form a customs union with nil tariff rates between its members.

In fact, the developing countries, at successive meetings of the United Nations Conference on Trade and Development (UNCTAD), have urged that they need positive discrimination in their favour. They have maintained that if they are to develop industries to the point where they will be on a big enough scale and operated with enough skill and experience to be competitive, they need to be able to protect their home markets from cheaper imports from the industrial countries. This is the infant industry argument, which has a respectable standing among economists, though as we shall see there is always the danger that the infants never grow up to the point where they can dispense with the protection.

At the same time, the developing countries also argue that if they are to build up exports which make use of their advantages of cheap labour, they need to be granted preferential access to the markets of the rich industrial countries. At present, while for instance the United States, the EEC countries and Japan normally admit basic primary materials duty free, they impose duties on these goods if they are processed before export, or made into manufactured goods. Thus the developing countries are penalized for trying to build up those industries which use their advantages of cheap raw materials and cheap labour.

There is a need for a change of attitude on the part of the rich countries. At present they tend to protect their labour-intensive industries, using imported raw materials like cotton and jute textiles, because of the danger of unemployment among those engaged in them. It would be to their long term advantage to import such goods more cheaply from countries with abundant cheap labour, and to retrain their more expensive labour for employment in industries which need greater technical skill or capital resources, like electronics or chemicals. They also tend to protect their own farmers in growing crops like sugar beet against competition from cheaper cane sugar from the Third World. The trouble is that such an adjustment would be painful in the short period because it would be concentrated on limited groups of people, such as the mill owners and mill workers of Lancashire or Dundee, or the French and German beet growers. These are often vocal and politically influential. The benefits from cheaper imports, on the other hand, would be dispersed over the whole body of consumers and hence are less appreciated.

So far, although the UNCTAD conferences have led to limited agreements to give preferences to imports from the developing countries, these have been so hedged around with exclusions and escape clauses that they have not brought them much benefit. There are some signs of progress, however, notably the Lomé agreement early in 1975 extending the preferential access to the EEC markets previously enjoyed by former French and Belgian colonial territories to a wide range of former British colonies.

But the developing countries themselves have not always pursued the wisest policies. Some of them, especially in Latin America, have put too much weight on protecting industries serving their own often very narrow home markets, rather than trying to encourage exports. Manufacturers have been given tariff protection, and favourable access to capital for investment and to imports of raw materials. Systems of exchange control have acted as a further protection, for they have led to currencies becoming overvalued at the official exchange rates, and this has further discouraged exports, while making it difficult for importers to get hold of foreign currency to finance imports. The result has been a growth of small, inefficient industries with markets too limited to enjoy the economies of scale. This has made consumer goods dearer, but benefited those engaged in the industries through high profits and relatively high wages, and thus built up vested interests in continued protection. There have been some attempts to get over the problem of limited markets, through customs unions like the Central American Common Market and the Latin American Free Trade Area. These have had little effect, however, since most of these countries' trade is with North America and Europe rather than with one another.

(*c*) *Foreign private investment and the multinational companies*

It is in connection with the development of wider sources of trade that the role of foreign private investment and of the multinational companies has come to prominence. International commercial investment is perhaps the most obvious way of building up new forms of production and hence new types of exports. Nowadays, it takes the form mostly of direct investment by companies based in one country acquiring or setting up plant in other countries, rather than the portfolio investment by private individuals buying the stock of foreign governments or shares in foreign enterprises, which was the usual pattern before 1914. Most international investment in manufacturing takes place in other industrial countries, rather than in the Third World, though some international companies have set up plant in some of the bigger countries, like India, Mexico or Brazil. In general international investment in the Third World is mostly in mines, plantations and oil wells.

Such investment has not been without its benefits to the host countries. It has provided a good deal of employment and training in basic skills. It has often led to substantial provision of infrastructure, such as roads, railways, ports, or power stations, as well as banking and insurance facilities. It has been a big source of new exports, of minerals, like copper or tin, iron or bauxite, or plantation products like tea, coffee, sugar or rubber, and hence a big foreign exchange earner. It has also been a very important source of taxation revenue to the governments concerned, often outweighing all others.

Yet there has been growing uneasiness in the Third World about the multinational companies. Though there is probably no other way in which the capital and knowhow could be made available to develop unused resources, yet too often the result has been the kind of dual economy described above, with profits going abroad, technical expertise coming from abroad, and little effect in stimulating local development. There has been a feeling that these companies are too powerful, influential and experienced relative to the governments they have to deal with. They are concerned inevitably with their own international interests rather than the welfare of their hosts, and their investment plans and operations are decided accordingly. It is felt that they can rig prices and wages to suit themselves and transfer profits to avoid taxation. There is complaint that they are only too prone to enlist the support of their home governments to bring pressure to bear against any regimes which seek to curb or control them.

All the same, governments in the Third World have shown that they can get their way if they are determined, and especially where they can take advantage of favourable market positions. The best example is that of the Organization of Petroleum Exporting Countries (OPEC). This was set up by the governments of countries controlling the cheapest, most abundant and most easily worked sources of oil, mostly in the Middle East, for instance in Saudi Arabia, Iran and the Gulf States, but also in Venezuela and Nigeria. The Arab-Israeli conflict gave the Arab states the motivation to act together, while their cost advantage and the dependence of the industrial world on their supplies enabled them to more than turn the tables on the tightly-knit group of international oil companies. Whereas these companies had taken advantage of their expertise and capital to ensure that they got the benefits of the profit margin between low oil extraction costs and higher selling prices, fixed to protect higher cost producers like the United States, the OPEC countries were able to bring about a five-fold rise in oil prices in 1973–74. A drop in demand since then, and the prospect of other sources of energy supply, has caused the market to sag, but it is unlikely that the balance of advantage will be reversed, since the producer countries are also acquiring the ownership of the oil well operations in their territories. This will enable them to cut back on the rate of extraction rather than allow prices to fall.

Similar advantages have been achieved by other countries which have controlled a low cost source of supply, in extracting for themselves the profit margin which this gives them. The copper producers have managed to come together with some success in a sellers' cartel, while the Zambian government has acquired a 51% share in the ownership of the copper mines in its territories. The Jamaican government also has been successful in getting high prices for its bauxite, of which it is a low cost producer, and the cane sugar producing countries were very successful in taking advantage of high world sugar demand in 1974–75.

The fact is that international companies are as dependent on the co-operation of the governments of the countries they work in, as the governments are on the companies for the supply of capital, markets and expertise. Governments always possess the ultimate threat of expropriation. If a government is strong and stable and knows what it wants, in the way of tax revenue, or a share in the higher posts in the company for its nationals, or an undertaking to plough back profits into further investment in the country, it can usually get it. The companies are concerned to have good relations for the sake of their image and for smooth operations and are generally prepared to negotiate.

(*d*) *Techniques and expertise*

As much of a bottleneck as the shortage of capital and of foreign exchange has been the shortage of technical skills of all kinds. Not only is there a lack of technologists trained in modern scientific methods, of teachers, research workers, agricultural experts, doctors, business executives and administrators with the skills and experience taken for granted in the West: there is a similar dearth of technicians to operate and maintain machinery, of clerks and typists and the whole vast range of subordinate skills which are needed for the operation of a modern economic and social system.

Hence a considerable part of the aid programme has consisted of technical assistance. This includes the provision of technical experts such as agriculturalists, engineers, doctors, chemists, administrators and teachers to advise the governments of developing countries on the best ways to make use of their resources, help with the setting up of universities, colleges and training centres in the developing countries, and provision for the training of their nationals in the industrial countries. The specialized agencies of the United Nations, such as the Food and Agricultural Organization (FAO), the World Health Organization (WHO) and the United Nations Educational, Scientific and Cultural Organization (UNESCO) have played a large part in this work.

Yet with resources so limited and needs so great there has been considerable criticism of mistaken policies and wasted effort. In education, for instance, there has been a tendency to give priority to extending basic literacy as quickly as possible and building upon this a superstructure of secondary and higher teaching very much in the pattern of Europe or North America. Many have urged that it would be better to give priority to training specialists in the skills which are most urgently needed, such as craftsmen who can operate modern machinery, and agriculturalists who can demonstrate modern methods to farmers.

In particular, the criticism has been that many of the least developed countries have tended to go straight for what they feel to be the best and most advanced of Western techniques and culture, rather than what is most appropriate to their own position. Thus one gets the rapid establishment of universities teaching courses in advanced physics and chemistry, or literature, or philosophy, aiming at the same standards as those of the West, and similarly of modern, lavishly equipped hospitals in the capital cities. Yet there may be a more urgent need for agricultural technicians who will work in the villages, or for technologists who can apply their knowledge of science to devising simple plant and machines using local materials and labour, or for simply trained medical orderlies who can staff rural clinics.

Education at the secondary and higher levels tends too often to be geared to producing a flood of white collar workers who want to leave the villages and seek jobs as lawyers or journalists or civil servants in the cities. So we get the paradox of acute shortages of certain key skills together with serious unemployment among the educated.

This links up with the problem hinted at above of the nature of the technical development appropriate to countries with large resources of labour and traditional skills, but an acute shortage of capital and modern technical expertise. It makes little sense to concentrate on the application of Western techniques of large-scale mechanized manufacturing and agriculture which are based on the opposite conditions of scarce labour and plentiful capital and technological skill.

Sometimes, of course, modern large-scale methods must be used. It makes sense for a country like India to develop its steel industry, for it has a very large population, a big industrial sector and plenty of coal and iron ore. By the same token it can appropriately develop modern engineering and chemicals; in fact, it is already a large exporter of engineering goods. Similarly, some types of technique have to be applied on a capital-intensive basis if they are to be viable. Electricity generation and fertilizer manufacture are usually in this category, while the Chinese experiments with backyard steel-making during the Great Leap Forward were not very successful.

Yet in general the great need is for an intermediate technology, that will use the plentiful labour force and its traditional skills and enable it to be more productive in ways which use little capital and not too complex techniques. An African farmer who uses only a hoe can often do better if he has a plough, or an Asian farmer with a wooden plough may get much better results with an iron one. Craftsmen like carpenters, metalworkers, weavers or shoemakers can be given better tools or small machines, perhaps power driven if electricity is available. By such means employment can be found in the rural areas for those displaced from the land as population grows and agricultural productivity rises, and the drift into idleness in the cities can hopefully be stemmed.

But in many cases the appropriate techniques do not yet exist, for modern technology both in agriculture and industry is geared to American and European conditions. A lot of effort needs to be put into research into the problems of small farmers in tropical climates, as well as into those of craftsmen and small-scale industrialists. Appropriate facilities for providing technical advice and credit are also necessary.

(*e*) *Political and social factors*

Increasingly, however, it is being realized that purely economic and technical measures are not enough to ensure development, if political and social factors are adverse. In many countries political power is in the hands of large landowners who have an interest in retaining the present system and little motive for changing it. They are often in a position to prevent any effective land reforms which would give the peasants security of tenure and fairer rents. They are often allied with the wealthy merchants and industrialists in keeping down taxation, and blocking social reforms. In other countries like many in Africa society is still basically tribal and politics tend to be a matter of rivalries between different tribes. In either case the personal following of particular leaders, or the seeking of favours for the benefit of one's own family and kin, tend to be more important than the clear-cut pursuit of political programmes.

Where a dominant social class is strongly entrenched, a political revolution to overthrow its power may be necessary before any effective reforms can take place. There is reason to believe that this is true, for instance, in much of Latin America and South-East Asia. The failure of Allende in Chile and of earlier democratic regimes in Uruguay, Brazil,

Venezuela, Peru and elsewhere points in this way. On the other hand, countries like Mexico and Bolivia which had revolutions earlier have shown that a radical regime can in time develop into a system of inequalities and injustices once the original zeal fades.

In such circumstances many look to the examples of China and Cuba, as showing how a regime with a strong ideology can provide the motive power and the enthusiasm to carry out a consistent programme of radical development, though at the expense of repression of opponents and enforcement of ideological conformity. There is good evidence, for instance, that China has gone a long way towards solving the problem of balanced development of agriculture and small industry, through its system of rural communes. It has also guaranteed an adequate food supply and prevented the drift of population to the towns.

There are also examples of other regimes which have achieved considerable success by less far-reaching methods. In city states like Hong Kong and Singapore rapid industrial and commercial growth has been achieved by free enterprise, though admittedly at the cost of considerable social injustice. Something similar has been true in Kenya, which though still basically a peasant country has had a lot of industrial and commercial development through free enterprise. In other cases right-wing authoritarian regimes have achieved rapid growth, as has happened in Brazil and also in Taiwan and South Korea, though in these circumstances there is apt to be a lot of political injustice. Frequently, military regimes have stepped in to oust corrupt and self-seeking politicians, and some of them have had constructive social and economic policies which they have pursued with considerable success, as in Nigeria and Peru. In other cases there has been a charismatic leader with more far-reaching and idealistic policies. The best example is President Nyerere in Tanzania, whose concept of village-based socialism has had wide appeal, but President Kaunda in Zambia has pursued somewhat similar lines also with success.

Stress is often laid on ideological obstacles to growth, such as a lack of social prestige and other incentives to business enterprise, or a spirit of fatalism arising from repeated experience of catastrophes, or a lack of concern about material riches. Traditional social attitudes, such as those embodied in caste in India can certainly be strong, but there is evidence that experience of the possibilities of growth can bring about appropriate changes of attitudes. For instance, the market traders and lorry owners of West Africa show abundant business enterprise, and so do certain Indian caste groups like the Marwaris, out of which the famous

Birla business clan has sprung. Nor would those who admire the Eastern philosophies with their emphasis on detachment from desires be happy at the prospect of this traditional wisdom giving place to rootless, restless Western materialism. Indeed this raises deeper issues of vital importance to the Christian, namely what kind of ideology does one need to achieve a concern for growth which is not based purely on individual selfishness, but on securing the best interests of the community as a whole.

4. *Policy consequences*

What conclusions can we draw from this survey of the present state of the developing world about the types of policy which we in the developed industrial countries should pursue? This has implications both for direct attitudes to the developing countries and for the general organization of the world trading and monetary system.

(*a*) *Aid is an end in itself*

Aid, if it is to be effective, must be advocated and sustained as an end in itself, for the benefit of the recipient countries rather than in the short-term interests of the donors. This may be difficult to sell to the electorate, but any other approach risks disillusion as well as lessening the effectiveness of the aid. Hence there should be a willingness to continue and increase the payments without expecting a *quid pro quo* in the shape of support by the recipient countries of policies believed to be in the donor's interest. The aid should be given as far as practicable in the form of grants or interest-free loans and should be untied. However, if it is not possible to get political support for untied aid, tied aid is better than none. In general, too, the donors should accept the programmes and priorities devised by the recipients, rather than trying to force on them their own ideas of what is appropriate.

Ultimately the only valid basis for advocating aid is the moral duty of the people of the rich countries to help those in the poor countries to help themselves. The argument of enlightened self-interest - in the benefits of a more prosperous and peaceful world - can be used if it is kept on a long-term basis. It is ultimately in the interests of the developed countries that the rest of the world should be prosperous, if only because prosperous countries are usually one another's best markets. But there should be no illusions about the short term. Development, and the rising expectations which it brings, is more likely to lead to political unrest and disturbance, as it breaks down the stagnation that so often accompanies extreme poverty. And in the short run too the countries of the Third World are as likely to prove rivals in trade as customers. They will develop industrial exports based on cheap labour which will undercut our labour-intensive types of goods. They will compete with us for supplies of food and raw materials and will try to organize to raise the prices of the primary products which they control.

(*b*) *Positive discrimination in trade and payments*

If the rich countries are to help the poorer countries to develop, they must be prepared to discriminate positively in their favour. They must be prepared to admit to their home markets those goods in which the developing countries have a comparative advantage, especially manufactures in which cheap labour is important and tropical agricultural products. They should not be too concerned to protect their own relatively inefficient industries, but should work out ways of redeploying labour and capital into industries in which they can make use of their own comparative advantage of greater technological skill and more abundant capital. This is ultimately to the gain of both parties.

At the same time, the rich countries must accept that the poorer countries will want to discriminate against their exports in order to build up industries in a protected market to the level at which they can enjoy the economies of scale. There is a danger that these infant industries will never grow up, but on the whole this must be accepted. They will also want to impose conditions on foreign firms investing in their territories, and often to take them into national or public ownership. Provided the terms on which this is done are fair, this too should be accepted.

There is also a need for the international monetary authorities to ensure that adequate means of international payment are made available to the developing countries. This problem has become more acute with the recent steep rise in oil prices. This has put an especially heavy burden on those poor countries, the majority, who are not themselves oil producers. Many of them are heavily dependent on oil as their main source of fuel and power, and the drain on their limited resources of foreign exchange is acute. The proposals for recycling the oil producers' surpluses at present being considered should include making sure that an adequate proportion of them is channelled to the developing countries. From time to time there have been proposals that more general schemes for improving world liquidity, through, for instance, expanding the flow of special drawing rights from the International Monetary Fund, should be implemented by making special advances to the developing countries, which could then use them to increase their imports from the industrial countries. This would both ease the payments problems of the Third World and encourage a general expansion of world trade, and should be favourably considered.

(*c*) *A long-term problem*

The problem of world development must be accepted as a long-term one, to which there is no quick or easy solution. The people of the developed countries will have to accept the need for a continuing policy of helping the Third World both in aid and trade, which if it is to be any good will be with us for the foreseeable future. Moreover, if such a policy is to be accepted, there is need for a sustained effort of public education, to help the people of the rich countries to understand the difficulty and complexity of the problems of development. It must be expected that, at best, progress will not be smooth. There will be political disturbances and the emergence of regimes which will adopt policies unpopular in the West. With the rise of incomes and opportunities, aspirations and expectations will also rise, so that countries undergoing development are likely to be less stable, rather than more stable, than those sunk in stagnant poverty.

But we in the rich world must remember that, whatever our governments do in the way of aid, and however this can be supplemented by the efforts of voluntary agencies like Oxfam, War on Want and Christian Aid, the great bulk of the effort and sacrifice must come from the people of the countries themselves. They are the ones who have to squeeze more savings out of their meagre incomes. They are the ones who have to undergo all the strains and stresses of the upheaval of old ways and the introduction of new ones. They are the ones who may be displaced from their villages and forced to seek a new life in crowded city slums.

(*d*) *A welfare world?*

Can we look forward to a welfare world analogous to the Welfare State? Within the national states of the developed world it is accepted that the community as a whole should provide a source of income for those who cannot earn an adequate one themselves, and reasonable equality of access to services like education and medical treatment. It is also accepted that special efforts should be made to encourage the growth of new industries and other sources of employment in those regions which are suffering from a decline of their basic industries and lack an adequate employment base. Is it reasonable to expect that something similar could develop in the world community?

There are obvious obstacles. There is no international organization with the authority and power to carry out such a welfare programme. Quite clearly the United Nations and its agencies, for all their achievements, do not at present have this position, and the sovereign states are most unwilling to consider giving it to them. More important, there is not the same feeling of community and mutual responsibility between nations as there is within one national state, with its common heritage of history and customs and usually free movement from one part to another. In particular, the gap in living standards, in culture, in experience, ideologies and ways of thought, between the people of the industrial countries of Western Europe and North America and those of Africa or Southern Asia, is very great indeed. In spite of television, we do not feel the same direct sense of responsibility for people very different from ourselves. There is also a feeling that the problem of world poverty and underdevelopment is so stupendous that it is not practicable to aim at the same sort of levelling up of standards which appears a reasonable aim within one homogeneous country. This feeling has been further enhanced in the last few years by doubts whether world resources will be adequate for growth on a scale sufficient to raise the living standards of the poor countries in this way, and also by fears of the effects of pollution.

These last issues we deal with in the next chapter. But meanwhile, however impracticable the welfare world may be as an immediate policy aim, as an ultimate ideal and criterion by which to judge policies, nothing else can be satisfactory to those who accept the Christian position that all men are brothers of equal value in the sight of God.

5. *What light can be thrown on the problem by the Christian understanding?*

(*a*) *Advocating generosity*

This last observation reminds us that this is a field in which above all there is a need for a continued attitude of altruism, not to say generosity. The governments and peoples of the rich countries are being called upon to introduce and sustain policies on aid and trade designed not primarily in their own interests, but in those of the disadvantaged majority of the world's population. Governments cannot do this in the absence of a climate of public opinion which supports it; the more so as there are always pressure groups calling for the reduction of overseas aid as a waste of money, or for protection against competition by imports from Third World countries.

There are many others besides those in the churches who are aware of this as a moral responsibility. Indeed the 'Aid Lobby' has been effective in ensuring that a modest programme of aid has been introduced and sustained in spite of continued economic and financial crises. But Christians have a special responsibility in this respect, since their faith teaches them to think of the interests of others as much as of their own, and in particular to consider the interests of the poorest and least advantaged. Those who take seriously St John's criticisms of people who say they love God, but see their neighbour hungry and do nothing about it (I John 3.17), or Jesus' warning that those who failed to minister to the ones in need were failing to minister to him (Matt. 25.41–45), cannot accept complacently a situation in which a minority of the world's people are in comfort, while the majority are in abject poverty.

(*b*) *The importance of knowledge*

For most of us most of the time, the needs of the developing world are a case of out of sight, out of mind. It is easy enough to forget about poverty among our own people, the old, the disabled, the unsupported mothers, the low earners with large families, the down-and-outs. But we do at least meet them from time to time and we all expect to be old ourselves. Most of us have little occasion to visit developing countries, and when we see pictures on television or read reports of living conditions in India or Africa, are inclined to feel that it is different for 'them'; after all, 'they' are used to it.

Here, Christians have an advantage and a responsibility through their membership of the world-wide church. Our own churches in Europe and North America are in close contact with the churches in Asia, Africa and Latin America. Foreign missions have traditionally given us an interest in them that has been real and sincere, even if often limited and paternalistic. Nowadays more and more we are thinking of mutual sharing of resources in doing God's work in the world and mutual learning from one another's experiences. Church men and women from the West go to work in the churches of the Third World, and church men and women from there come to work here.

Through this mutual sharing Christians in Britain, for instance, if they are imaginative and sympathetic, have the means of seeing into the life of ordinary men and women in Kenya, or Nigeria or India. They can in imagination live the life of the people, face their problems, share their aspirations.

The churches and their members should thus be a source of authentic knowledge about the life of the people of the Third World and the way they feel and think and act. They have the responsibility of sharing this insight with their fellow-countrymen who do not have these contacts.

(*c*) *Realism and persistence*

From these contacts there should come a greater realism and a greater persistence. The more we know about the countries of the developing world and the more contact we have with their people, the more we shall realize the complexity of the problems which they face, and the more we shall be able to help our own fellow countrymen to understand that there are no easy and simple solutions. Moreover, Christian experience ought to make such realism come more easily to us. We know that our motives are mixed and can understand that other people's motives are mixed also. We know that what we are and how we think and act is very much influenced by our background and experience and can appreciate that this, too, is true of others.

We will therefore not look for over-simplified explanations. The trouble is not all due to exploitation by wicked capitalists in the West and the machinations of international companies. Nevertheless, historical circumstances have led us to a situation where all of us in the rich countries, business men, professional people, manual workers, governments alike benefit disproportionately from the ordinary terms of intercourse through trade and financial transactions with the people of the developing countries. Similarly, the problem is not to be blamed simply on rapacious landowners and corrupt governments in the developing countries, nor on a spirit of apathy and lack of enterprise among the bulk of their populations. Yet once again, historical circumstances have led to a situation where these reactions are all too evident. Still less can the whole thing be written off as due to Communist agitators stirring up trouble, though it is not surprising that Marxist explanations and Marxist remedies find much credence among the more articulate in the Third World.

So we will not have any great hopes of a quick and easy solution through some simple change of policy, such as more aid, or ending aid tying, or changing the rules about trade discrimination. We will be ready to look more deeply and radically at the whole terms of the relationship between developed and developing countries and to advocate bold policies to change it, should these seem desirable. At the same time, we will avoid the fatalism that argues that nothing worth while can be done without an unlikely revolution. We will know and help others to see that many types of policy must be tried, and that the next step is always worth taking, provided we have thought out as best we can the effects it is likely to have. We will thus be ready to continue doing what seems to be right in the knowledge that it is worth doing, even if its results are limited, provided there is flexibility to adapt our policies to changing circumstances.

(*d*) *All members of one world*

Finally, Christians should find it easier to realize what it means that this is one world, in which we are all members one of another. If people in some parts of the world are rich and others poor, the responsibility for dealing with this situation is not merely a simple matter of the rich helping the poor. It raises deep questions about the way of life, the ideals and values of both.

We have already seen the poor countries are poor because their economies are relatively unproductive, and this reflects a whole complex of factors about dependence on subsistence agriculture, social and political structures, attitudes to change and so on. The rich countries are rich because their economies are more productive, and this also involves many complexities about the ways in which this enables them to get hold of the world's resources on more favourable terms, and the motivation which makes the pursuit of material riches the dominant driving force in life.

The gap between rich and poor in the world today is so great as to make mutual understanding very difficult. It makes a mockery of the ideal of mankind as one community in which all men are to be seen as brothers, engaged in the mutual meeting of one another's needs. It is on these grounds that the Christian conscience cannot accept it. A century and a quarter ago Disraeli condemned the division of Britain into two nations of rich and poor who could not understand each other. We have done much to alleviate this, but now we are faced with two worlds, and geographical separation makes misunderstanding even more serious.

But to solve the problem of world poverty we will have to make a more responsible and more constructive use of the world's physical and human resources than we have yet done. Until recently, though most recognized the difficulty of doing this, few questioned its possibility in principle.

But in the last few years many of those concerned with the future of the environment have done just that. They question whether the supply of natural resources is adequate to enable all men to attain to a level of income comparable to that enjoyed in the rich countries, and they question whether the environment can stand up to the degree of pollution which the attempt to do so would involve. If this is true, the implications are obviously very serious, and so the next chapter is devoted to a fuller examination of the whole question of growth and the environment.

6

Growth and the Environment

1. *Is continued growth desirable or possible?*

Economic growth, in the sense of an increasing flow of goods and services becoming available to meet the community's wants, has been the dominant feature of economic life for the last two hundred years. In the developed world, it has made it possible for the bulk of ordinary men and women to break out of immemorial poverty and attain a standard of living hitherto only available to the privileged few. In the developing world it is the means on which hopes are fixed of following in the same path.

Until recently, though some have criticized its dangers in breeding self-seeking, materialism and greed, few have questioned its feasibility or even its fundamental desirability. But there has now come about a marked change.

The feasibility of continued economic growth has been questioned on three main grounds:

First, that world population growth is likely to outstrip the growth of food supply so that hopes of a rising standard of living will be dashed by the impossibility of feeding everyone adequately.

Secondly, that a continued growth of output involves a continued increase in the supply of resources and in particular non-renewable resources like metal ores and fossil fuels.

Thirdly, that the process of expanding both the food supply and the exploitation of natural resources, together with the growth of industrialism and urbanism, will lead to a massive increase in pollution of the environment and a possible breakdown of the eco-system on which life on earth depends.

The raising of these questions about feasibility has led also to growing doubts about the desirability of continued growth, and in particular the break-up of balanced communities with a satisfactory way of life, and their replacement by a striving after gain leading to general dissatisfaction, greed and conflict and a failure to achieve the things which are really worth while.

We must go into these arguments in detail, but first we must clarify what we mean by growth and then attempt a general assessment of the advantages and disadvantages which arise from its pursuit.

2. *What is growth?*

The economist means by growth an increase in the flow of material goods and services becoming available each year to the population, to be used either for consumption, or for investment in improving productive capacity. It is normally measured in terms of the gross national product of a country each year, corrected for price changes. To make possible comparisons over time and space, the total is usually related to the size of the population, so that the measure becomes the gross national product per head.

(*a*) *The gross national product*

The gross national product is the sum total of the value of all the final goods and services produced in a country in a year, to which a money value can be given. It includes only those goods and services which are used for final consumption or investment, and not those which form inputs for later stages of production. In other words, if we take the output of shirts, we include the value of all the shirts sold in the shops, but we do not include separately the value of the yarn, cloth, transport and handling costs at each stage, since these are all included in the final total. The total of the gross national product equals that of gross national income, which is the sum of the wages, salaries, profits, interest and rents earned in the process of creating the product. It also equals the gross national expenditure, which is the sum of all the end uses of the product, such as private consumption, investment in capital formation, government expenditure on services like education or defence, and exports minus imports.[1]

(*b*) *The limited significance of this measure*

When we say that gross national product per head is growing at, say 2% or 5% a year, we have to be very clear about the limited significance of what we are saying.

There are certain conventions about what we include in our measure.

We normally put in all those goods and services which are valued in cash, but not those which are not. In particular, we do not include the unpaid work of housewives and others in their homes, important though this is for welfare. Nor do we include unpaid charitable or public service work. In fact the only unpaid items normally included are the value of agricultural products consumed on farms, and the imputed annual value to owner-occupiers of the services they get from their houses. Also excluded are what are called transfer incomes, such as pensions and others forms of social security, since these do not correspond to any additional flow of product of labour or capital by their recipients, but are merely a transfer of income from taxpayers to beneficiaries.

The inclusion of goods and services in the national product thus implies that people are prepared to pay for them, either by buying them in the market, or through taxation and public spending, and that resources have to be used up to provide them. But this does not necessarily mean that the value placed on them represents an increase of well-being to the community. In many cases they reflect a use of resources to counteract evils rather than to provide positive benefits. This is true of a great deal of public spending, on defence, law and order, sewerage and refuse collection and the like. It is also true of a good deal of private spending on travel to and from work, or soundproofing of houses against traffic or aircraft noise. These represent the price we have to pay for the advantages of living in a modern urban society as against a simpler, poorer rural one.

By and large the figures which go into the gross national product represent what economists call private costs and benefits, rather than social costs and benefits. They measure the price which we have to pay in the shops, which in turn reflects the costs which the manufacturers and distributors have to meet, for labour, raw materials, depreciation on plant, transport, handling and so on. These do not include any social costs which do not fall on the producers or the consumers, but on the community as a whole, such as pollution of the atmosphere by fumes and of rivers by effluents, noise, traffic congestion, the nervous strain of working in factories and so on. Nor does it include any social benefits which are enjoyed not by the person paying for the goods or services, but by the community as a whole, such as the reduction of congestion caused when people travel to work by train or bus instead of by private car, or the benefits which the community gets from having better standards of education and health, as distinct from those enjoyed by individual students or patients.

Some of these social costs may not fall on the present generation, but may be passed on to the future. Any adverse effects on future generations of the exhaustion of mineral resources, or of the eroding of fertility by unsound agricultural methods, or a cumulative growth of pollution, would be of this kind. On the other hand, benefits from improved education and health services, or better standards of nutrition, or from effective methods to reduce pollution, will in part be passed on to future generations also.

Even when we have adjusted our measure to take account of the 'bads', such as urban congestion or the rise of crime, which have to be set against many of the so-called 'goods', and of those 'goods' which escape our yardstick, all we are measuring is the size of the flow of new material goods and services becoming available to the community to make use of. We are saying nothing about the relationship between growth and welfare. We are not implying that a country whose real national product is growing at the rate of 5% a year is somehow 5% happier or more satisfied or more virtuous each year.

In the first place, we have to take account of how the product is shared out. It is possible, and we have seen that in some of the developing countries this has happened, that most of the extra product is going to a few rich people and the bulk of the population is getting little or no benefit from it. Most of us would probably want to say that a fast rate of growth, coupled with extreme and growing inequality of income, is less satisfactory in terms of welfare than a slower rate of growth, accompanied by a more equal distribution. To say this involves a value judgment, for we cannot know objectively that the extra enjoyment of the rich does not outweigh the misery of the poor, but it is a value judgment which most would find acceptable.

This reminds us that value judgments are inevitable if we are to get from our measure of gross national product to any concept of changes in social welfare. We cannot know that a modern industrial society, in which most of the people are well-fed, well-clothed, well-educated and in good health is in any absolute sense 'better' than a poor peasant or tribal society. The simpler, rural society may give more in the way of contentment through belonging to a community in which everyone has his place, as against the restless striving of urban life. On the other hand the urban society opens up wider opportunities and offers more varied experience.

3. *The advantages and disadvantages of growth*

Nevertheless, there are certain things which we can say about the general effects, good and bad, of a fairly fast and steady growth in the output of material goods. It will be useful to run through these before going on to consider the three question marks about its feasibility in more detail.

(a) Advantages

1. The main advantage of growth is that more material resources give us more opportunities of deciding how to use them, more choices as to the wants and needs to be met. But we have to decide how to use them.

In the first place we can raise living standards generally. Even in the rich countries there are still many who cannot enjoy the comfortable way of life which most middle-class people take for granted, with spacious and well-furnished homes, long holidays, opportunities for travel, sport, culture and the arts. Most people are not so well off that they could not get real satisfaction out of a higher standard of living. And as we saw in chapter 4, large numbers, several million in Britain, among the retired, the chronic sick, unsupported families and low-paid workers, can barely afford the minimum poverty level regarded as adequate by the community. They cannot be sure of enough food and warmth, still less of decent housing.

2. We have a choice about the means we use to distribute the increased product. Some of it can be disposed of through the market, by enabling people to earn higher real wages and salaries and spend them on buying more of what they choose. Some of it can be used, communally, by increasing government spending on schools, health services, social services and social security, or environmental services like roads and urban redevelopment. A rising real national product makes it easier to redistribute a bigger share to those who are less well off, and also to use a bigger share to provide services to be enjoyed by the community as a whole, like sports facilities, theatres, art galleries, parks and other amenities, or measures to combat pollution.

3. A rising real national product also makes it easier, given the will, to undertake redistribution internationally. If there is general prosperity and living standards are rising in the industrial countries, it is easier to get political support for generous aid programmes and also for the entry of imports of cheap manufactures from the developing countries. If the

industrial countries are prosperous, they are also better markets for the raw materials and foodstuffs exported from the Third World. Against this, however, must be set the adverse effect of inflation in the rich countries on the prices of the manufactured goods which they export to the developing countries.

4. Moreover, a mixed economy such as ours undoubtedly works better in a climate of growth than in one of stagnation or decline. Growth provides the profits which are the motive for business firms to undertake new enterprise, developing more productive processes and new types of product. Profits also provide the resources out of which new investment can be carried out. Growth means full employment and rising real earnings and thus makes it easier to get men to move to new jobs and accept labour saving methods. Growth provides the government with a rising tax revenue which enables it to expand the provision of public services without having to put up tax rates.

All these advantages are operational rather than moral in character. It is a fact that our economy works more smoothly if it is growing. It is a fact that a growing economy gives the opportunity to make most of the people better off in real terms, provided the increased product is used wisely. It is a fact that it makes it easier to share some of the growth with countries which are less well off. But if the offsetting disadvantages are thought to outweigh these advantages, then it is up to us to find ways of making the economy work smoothly without the stimulus of growth. Let us therefore look at the disadvantages.

(*b*) *Disadvantages*

Like all choices in economic life, that of growth has its costs. If we give priority to growth, we may have to sacrifice other aims.

1. To get a faster rate of economic growth, we may have to sacrifice security. Business firms must be prepared to give up safe and tried forms of production and risk capital in new and untried processes and products. They may make big profits, but they risk big losses. Some firms will be successful and will grow and take over other firms; others will be less successful and will lose out in competition and either go bankrupt or be taken over. Their directors and top managements risk demotion or the golden handshake. Workers at all levels risk having their skills made obsolete by new methods and having to change their jobs, or perhaps if they are getting on being unable to find new jobs. They cannot continue in the comfortable routine of doing the same job in the same way, in the same place, with the same colleagues, year after

year. The strain and stresses of insecurity must be set against the excitement of change and the bigger material rewards which growth can bring.

2. A more rapid growth involves the risk of greater damage to the environment. There may have to be more rapid exploitation of mineral deposits, with the damage that mine workings can do to the scenery, the atmosphere and the water. New industrial processes may involve uncertain risks of harmful or unpleasant effluents. Industry may have to grow in unspoiled areas of the countryside, and decay in other areas, leaving dereliction behind it.

On the other hand, a more rapid growth gives more resources to combat pollution. The community can afford to spend more on cleaning up rivers and the atmosphere, it can afford to make firms take more care to stop pollution, it can insist on the restoration of derelict sites and control the exploitation of new ones.

3. In the short run, we may have to sacrifice other aims, such as greater equality. As we saw in chapter 4, in the short run, if our first priority is growth, we may have to allow firms to make big profits and pay high salaries to top management, and go easy on taxation to avoid disincentives. This may mean less scope for spending more on pensions and other aid to the poor, education, health services, housing and so on, or for that matter on roads, pollution control or defence.

In the long run, however, growth makes it possible to spend more on these things, because it gives us a bigger cake to cut up.

4. There are also a number of less tangible disadvantages of growth which are often stressed, such as the encouragement of a rootless, restless materialism, discontent, greed, envy, going all out for the main chance, ruthless disregard for those trampled on, and the like.

To a large extent these reflect a conflict of values. How far is it a 'good thing' that men and women should be encouraged to 'get on', do the best they can to use their talents to build up a position in life, to create and run a successful business giving large-scale employment and meeting the community's wants more efficiently? How far is it 'better' that they should be contented with their lot, make a modest living doing a conscientious job, cultivate their gardens, enjoy their neighbour's company, even if it means missing opportunities to use their talents to the full? There is always the problem of how to reconcile the spirit of energy and ambition, which wants to get things done, with the spirit of contentment and humble and loving service.

Some of the forms which this conflict takes arise out of the nature of our society and economic system. In a market system the pursuit of growth demands business success and that in turn means promoting a demand for one's goods by all the methods of modern advertising, product differentiation, competitive innovation and the like. Firms have to invest large amounts of capital in plant to make new products which will come on the market later, and hence they have to create a demand for them before the public have been able to appreciate them. There is thus a built-in incentive to stimulate new demands, to make people feel that they must have the latest sensation in detergents, cosmetics or chocolates, that their old car or television set is obsolete and they must have a new one. This sort of commercialism, so much criticized of late, is an undoubted cost of the rapid rise in real income which we have enjoyed in the industrial countries.

In other countries, like those of Eastern Europe, the costs have been different. In the centrally planned economies the emphasis has been on building up basic capital goods industries by direct government action, and the consumers have had to take second place and make do with what is available. There has been no need for consumer promotion, rather empty shelves and limited choice and long queues.

Such is the list of advantages and disadvantages. Before attempting to strike a balance and to see what light Christian understanding can throw on our priorities in doing so, we must first look at the three great obstacles to feasibility listed in section 1 above.

4. *The challenge to the continued feasibility of growth – (1) Population and food supply*

The first challenge to the continued feasibility of growth comes from the prospect of population growth outstripping food supply.

(*a*) *The world population position*

The developing world is going through the population phase which the developed world experienced during the last century, but at a much faster rate. The spread of medical knowledge, and in particular the control of the large-scale epidemic diseases, has produced a dramatic drop in mortality, so that crude death rates[2] have commonly dropped from 30 or 40 per thousand of the population to, say, 15 per thousand or less in the course of ten or twenty years. Fertility rates, based on past experience of heavy infant and child mortality, are still high, with the crude birth rate[2] still up at 35 to 40 per thousand. The result is rapid population growth, often at rates of up to 3% a year, and a very young population, with families of five or six or more, now mostly growing to maturity. So the prospects are for continued rapid population growth, because of the very large numbers of young couples starting their families, even if they could be induced to limit the number of their children.

By contrast, the developed countries are coming near to reaching stability. Their death rates have fallen to 10 per thousand, more or less, according to variations in age composition.[2] Their birth rates have fluctuated more markedly, because of changes in age of marriage and in family spacing, but have tended to fall towards a level not much higher, with average family size now only a little over two.

Thus Western Europe and North America and similar developed areas are not likely to make much contribution to the overall increase of world population. Their importance in this argument is that each West European or North American makes much greater demands on world resources of food, fuel, minerals and so on, than does each Asian or African.[3]

The upshot is that world population is expected to double from about 3,000 million in 1960 to over 6,000 million by the year 2000, even with a vigorous programme to encourage family limitation in the developing countries. Experience in the West suggests that the best hope of inducing an eventual levelling off rests on making it possible for people in the poorer countries to enjoy a higher and more secure standard of living. Once people come to realize that they do not need to have ten children to guarantee that some will survive to support them in later life, and that there is some prospect of their being able to give their children a better start than they could have themselves, then they will begin to want to limit their numbers so as to do better for each one.

The question is, have we enough margin of resources, especially food supply, to make this a realistic hope?

(*b*) *The world food supply problem*

During the 1960s it looked as if world food supply was keeping ahead of world population growth. Admittedly, the big increases in output came in the developed countries, notably in the United States and Canada, but also in Western Europe. But in the developing world also the effect of the Green Revolution seemed to be changing the position in the late sixties, especially in Asia. Thus India's food output in 1968–69 was about 10% higher than the previous record figure. Pakistan increased its wheat production by 50% in two years, Ceylon its rice production by 34% in the same length of time.[4]

In the early seventies these hopes seemed to be largely dashed. The Green Revolution had disappointed its proponents. The new strains of wheat and rice and maize needed costly irrigation and massive injections of fertilizers and could really only be grown by the big farmers. Rapid spread of irrigation itself produces problems, through the salination of the soil if the water is not properly drained away. Many parts of the world remain very vulnerable to droughts, and the rains have failed in many places recently, notably in India and Pakistan, in the Sahel area of West Africa south of the Sahara, and right across to Ethiopia and to parts of Kenya and Tanzania in East Africa. Alternatively, there may be sudden heavy rains and disastrous floods, as in parts of India, Pakistan and Bangladesh. Even some parts of the United States have suffered from these weather fluctuations.

Meanwhile, to ease the burden on the American Treasury of support payments to farmers, the stockpiles of grains in the United States which formed the world's main reserves have been allowed to run down, with the help of the Soviet Union, which made large wheat purchases from America to offset poor harvests at home. Consequently in 1975 we had a situation in which there were only a few weeks' reserves of the main grains available to meet the kind of disasters which droughts and floods are always likely to bring. And most of the available supplies tend to be bought by the rich countries, which alone can afford to pay for them, and are often used largely for fattening animals for meat.

There is little doubt that the world food supply problem could be solved. There is enough agricultural land, actual or potential, and enough technical knowledge available, to make it possible to feed a world population reaching 6,000 million by the year 2000, at a standard much higher than most people can attain today.

There is plenty of land still not cultivated, especially in Latin America, most of Africa and even in Asia apart from the Indian subcontinent. China has shown what can be done already if the energies and enthusiasm of the peasants can be harnessed to appropriate new methods. The periodic famines which used to ravage parts of the country are things of the past. If the level of output per acre throughout the developing world could be raised to that which is general practice in Western Europe and North America, the problem would be solved.[5] A great deal also could be done to reduce the loss of food in storage through rats, insects and weather, if proper granaries could be provided and pest control improved.

To say this, of course, is merely to state the problem. The techniques used in the West, the use of tractors and combine harvesters, high grade seeds and animals, intensive use of chemical fertilizers and pesticides, the application of applied science by the farmers to all their operations – these cannot just be transplanted to Asia or Africa. Many of them are not suitable. Tropical climates and tropical soils need different types of plants and animals; tropical rainstorms and heat can cause disastrous erosion if the wrong methods are used. African or Asian peasants have not the training nor the experience to use tractors and other complicated machinery, or unfamiliar crop rotations. They cannot afford elaborate irrigation or intensive use of chemical fertilizers. The rise in oil prices makes all these things even more expensive. In any case, where there is plenty of labour and little capital or science-based technical skill, it is extremely wasteful to use such methods.

What is needed is a sustained effort to develop forms of improved agricultural practice suitable to the conditions and the experience of farmers in each area concerned. This will involve, for instance, improved tools and equipment of a suitable kind, irrigation by wells and small dams where appropriate, devising of strains of plants and animals suited to the climate and other conditions, greater use of organic fertilizers like manure and household waste. It will also mean the provision of agricultural advisers willing to live in the villages and able to get the confidence of farmers, improved credit facilities, perhaps the organizing of co-operatives. In many cases, to be fully effective, it will mean changes in land tenure to give the farmers security. Hence it may be difficult to carry out such programmes without drastic political changes.

As agricultural productivity rises, and as population increases, a smaller proportion of the people can find support directly from the land. Hence the importance of developing other forms of employment, such as small-scale industries and crafts, or public services, to give a livelihood to those displaced, enabling them both to buy food for themselves and make a valuable contribution to the economy.

In the long run, then, food production can be increased to outstrip population growth, though it will not be easy. It will need well thought out and sustained programmes of rural development by all the countries concerned, together with world-wide measures to raise the level of incomes throughout the Third World.

For the immediate short run, the need is to rebuild reserves of grains and other basic foods, and to provide the means of distributing them quickly and efficiently to areas threatened with famine. There is a need to ensure not only that food reaches the countries concerned in adequate quantities, but that it can be distributed to the people throughout the affected countrysides and towns, where transport facilities are often poor and there is a danger of losses through weather, pests or peculation. There is also the problem of payment. The countries often lack foreign exchange to buy food in times of shortage, while the hungry people have no money to buy it on the market, even when it is made available. Efficient rationing schemes may be needed, but these depend on efficient administration.

The World Food Conference at Rome in November 1974 marked an international recognition of the problem. It did little, however, to lay down effective means of dealing with it.

Meanwhile, a solution will still depend on bilateral arrangements between governments, and supplies of the main food grains remain critically short. It is therefore not surprising that attention has been focussed on the extent to which world grain supplies are used up in the rich countries for fattening livestock. Rising incomes in the West mean higher meat consumption. Within the United States vast quantities of wheat, barley and maize are used to feed livestock to satisfy this demand. Of the grains which are available for world trade, disproportionate amounts go to those rich countries which are not self-sufficient in cereals and can afford to buy them up. Thus Japan, the United Kingdom, Italy and West Germany, with 7% of the world's population between them, recently accounted for 41% of world grain imports, whereas China and India together, with 36% of world population, only accounted for 13%.[6]

(c) *Conclusions on population and food supply*

Our conclusion must be that the world has the potential resources to feed the prospective increase in population, provided we use our knowledge, capital, skills and land effectively. If experience in the West is anything to go by, world population will eventually level off, when assurance of higher living standards leads to general family limitation.

For the meantime, a three-pronged approach must be used. There must be as much encouragement of family planning and family limitation as possible, but because of the deep-seated sentiments and beliefs which have to be overcome, progress in this is unlikely to be fast, unless living standards are felt to be rising. There must be vigorous efforts to encourage increased production of food in the developing world for they will have to face the main burden of meeting their own needs. There must also be a sustained effort to bring about a general expansion of output and incomes through the whole economies of the developing countries, to overcome the vicious circle of poverty which inhibits the expansion of their agriculture and industry and makes it so difficult for them to hold their own in world markets against the competition of the rich nations. The rich countries in turn will have to be more willing to make available surplus supplies of grain and other foods, and also provide the poor countries with some means of paying for it.

Given all this, the problem is soluble, though it will be touch and go for the next few years.

5. *The challenge to the continued feasibility of growth – (2) World resources*

(a) The possibility of exhaustion of resources

The second alleged obstacle to continued growth is pressure on world supplies of resources of raw materials and fuel. Consumption per head of these in the developed countries, with only a third of the world's population, is many times higher than it is in the developing world. For instance, steel consumption per head in the United States in 1969 was 682 kg., in Japan 603 kg. and in Britain 438 kg. But in India it was 11 kg. in China 21 kg. and in Nigeria only 7 kg.[7] Similarly, energy consumption per head in 1969 was 10·6 tons coal equivalent in North America and 3·5 tons in Western Europe, but only 0·3 tons coal equivalent in Africa and 0·4 tons in most of Asia.[8]

If Asia, Africa and Latin America develop their industries and living standards on the Western pattern and rise towards similar resource consumption levels, will available supplies be sufficient to support this? The more so if Western consumption figures continue to grow at recent rates?

We must distinguish between animal and vegetable materials, like timber, cotton, rubber, wool or leather, on the one hand, and minerals like iron, copper, tin, coal, oil or uranium on the other. The first type is renewable, and the problems with them are more akin to those of food supply, that is, problems of efficient farming. The destructive cutting down of natural forests, for instance, must give way to the controlled harvesting and replanting of timber. This is already being done in Britain and Scandinavia, if not yet in North America or the tropics.

More prominent have been the arguments about non-renewable mineral resources. These have been developed in a number of recent studies. The most notable is the report by Meadows and associates entitled *The Limits to Growth*, sponsored by the Club of Rome,[9] which deals also with population and food supply and with pollution. The method used was to take the latest available estimates of world reserves of the main minerals, and compare them with recent annual growth rates in consumption of them. Projecting the latter forward, estimates were made of how long reserves would last before becoming exhausted.

Extrapolating recent growth rates exponentially in this way, it was not difficult to show that on these assumptions, we would run out of most minerals within about fifty years, and to deduce that if this was so, economies based on rates of growth involving such use of resources would be faced with sudden collapse.

A popular summary of the arguments in the Report is to be found in the Penguin *A Blueprint for Survival*, first published in 1972 as an issue of *The Ecologist*.[10]

(*b*) *The feedback effects of demand for resources*

It has been fairly easy for economists, and indeed many natural scientists also, to point out the fallacies of this kind of simplified approach. By assuming fixed reserves and a continuance of current rates of growth of annual consumption, it ignores the feedback effects of rising demand in stimulating alternative sources of supply and encouraging more economical use.

1. In the first place, the known reserves of minerals are not a static figure. It is not worth while prospecting for and proving reserves beyond a reasonable amount at any time, and over the years known reserves have more than kept pace with the rapid rise in consumption. Thus over a century ago W. S. Jevons predicted that reserves of coal would be exhausted in about sixty years, whereas the world's known reserves are now thought to be adequate for several hundred years at much higher rates of use. Professor Beckerman has quoted a number of similar examples. For instance, in 1945 known copper reserves were 100 million tonnes. In the following 25 years, 93 million tonnes were mined, but at the end of the period, known reserves had increased to 300 million tonnes. Similarly with zinc, of which known reserves were 63 million tons in 1949, production between then and 1970 75 million tons, and reserves at the later date still larger than at the earlier. Iron ore reserves in 1944 were estimated at about 190 thousand million tonnes, but in 1971 were held to be probably over 200 thousand million tonnes. Coal reserves in 1913 were estimated at about 8,000 thousand million tonnes, and in 1967 at about 24,000 thousand million tonnes.[11]

The fact is that as the consumption of minerals grows, so new unknown resources are discovered, while new techniques make it possible to work profitably resources which were not workable earlier.

2. This leads on to the second point, that the process of increased consumption and pressure on the sources of supply itself brings into play a whole series of corrective mechanisms.

First, the pressure of demand will cause the price of the mineral to rise. This encourages the search for new and unknown deposits of it. It also makes it worth while to work deposits previously unprofitable because of remoteness and high transport costs, or poor quality of the ore, or difficulty of extraction. Thus the rise in Middle East oil prices has made it profitable to work the costly North Sea oil, and if prices continue high, it may become worth while exploiting oil shales and tar sands.

Secondly, technical progress which is always taking place is further stimulated by price rises. This makes it economical to develop resources previously unworkable; thus, for instance, it may soon be possible to use the vast deposits of minerals contained in nodules on the ocean beds. It also makes possible ever greater economy in the use of resources, so that more of the final output of metal or energy can be got out of a given input of ore and fuel. Improvements in the technique of iron and steel working have been continuously reducing the quantity of iron ore and coal needed to produce a ton of usable steel. Modern diesel and electric engines are much more economical of fuel than old-fashioned steam engines. A modern electricity generating station has a thermal efficiency half as large again as that of the stations in use at the end of the war, but since only about a third of the energy potential in the fuel finds its way into electrical energy, there is plenty of scope for further development.

Thirdly, pressure of demand, together with technical progress, also lead to the development of substitutes. Thus it is now possible to make use of the world's vast reserves of bauxite, so that aluminium, which was once a rare luxury, has become an increasingly cheap and common substitute for other metals such as copper in electrical work, or steel in the motor industry, box making and light construction work. In spite of its technical difficulties and its possible pollution risks, nuclear power has become a viable substitute for coal or oil in electricity generation. Other possibilities like nuclear fusion or the direct use of solar energy have yet to be developed.

Particularly prominent in recent decades has been the development of synthetics. Synthetic rubber is now superior to natural rubber for many purposes. Natural textiles like cotton, wool, jute and hemp are increasingly blended with or replaced by synthetics like nylon and terylene, while plastics have a very wide range of use from wrapping to furniture, car bodies to construction work.

Fourthly, pressure of demand on supplies gives an incentive to economy through recycling. When materials are cheap, a great amount of used products is wasted, from tin cans and scrapped cars to packaging materials and newspapers, because it does not pay to incur the heavy cost of collecting, sorting and re-using them. Most of this waste could be re-used comparatively easily if it were financially worth while to do so, and rising prices provide a stimulus to the setting up of organizations to handle the recycling. Many charities benefited from the high price of wood pulp in 1974, which made it well worth while to collect waste paper, only to have their hopes dashed again when paper prices fell and collecting ceased to pay.

(c) The prospects for resources

Although it remains formally true that the world's resources of non-renewable materials are finite, whereas potential demand can be extrapolated astronomically, it does not seem likely that resource supply will be a limiting factor to growth in the way often predicted by environmentalists.

In particular, there will not be a cumulative using up of 'known' reserves through an exponential continuance of present annual rates of growth of use, until the world economy comes to a sudden stop when some key resources, like iron, or oil, are used up. Rather the feedback mechanisms will ensure a continuous process of discovery of new natural resources, more effective exploitation of already known ones, substitution of cheaper alternatives for scarce materials, technical progress in developing new resources and economizing in old ones, development of synthetic substitutes and recycling of used materials.

It is true that the demand on world resources implicit in the raising of the living standards of the two-thirds of the world's population living in Asia, Africa and Latin America to the level of consumption prevailing in North America and Western Europe would, with existing techniques, make enormous demands. Particularly this is true in the field of energy, for increased energy input is implicit in nearly all forms of technical progress. But there is a counteracting tendency towards fuel economy, and plenty of scope to carry this further if energy becomes relatively dearer. And although limited oil supplies and higher oil prices will probably slow down the use of this most flexible of energy sources, this process will be more gradual than is often thought. Other sources such as coal and nuclear power are abundantly available, not to mention the possibilities of fusion and direct solar energy.

Resources, then, are likely to be adequate for the foreseeable future, and the feedback mechanisms will ensure that increasing demand produces an appropriate response of supply. As to the longer term future, we cannot usefully say very much. While we have a certain responsibility to exercise stewardship for our descendants, it is an open question how far we have an obligation to sacrifice the chance of a better living standard for the present generation on their behalf. This is the more so as experience suggests that human skill and ingenuity is more versatile in finding a solution to problems than we sometimes are prepared to admit. One proviso which must be made is that we have an obligation in meeting our needs today, not to do anything which does irreparable harm to the environment in which our successors must live, and that we must deal with in the next section.

However, there is no reason why growth should mean that consumption of non-renewable resources must continue to expand at recent rates. The developing countries need not raise their living standards by the same pattern of large-scale urbanized industrialization as the present developed world followed. Indeed the emphasis is more likely to come to be on small-scale intermediate technology using largely locally available materials and human power and aimed at keeping people in the countryside.

At the same time, in the developed world, living standards have reached the point where a further increase in well-being depends more on services than on goods. People in Europe and North America will want increasingly to consume more leisure services, such as sports, entertainments and cultural activities, and more public services, like education, medical treatment and social welfare. Services, whether privately or publicly provided, are essentially labour intensive and make relatively little use of raw materials, even when they employ sophisticated techniques based on computers and electronic visual aids.

6. *The challenge to the continued feasibility of growth – (3) Pollution and the environment*

In principle, then, world food supply could be increased fast enough to keep pace with rising population, and resource supply need not be a barrier to continued growth of world output. It should be possible, therefore, for living standards to rise enough to induce a general limitation of family size and hence a stabilization of population.

But what about the dangers of pollution? Will not a continued expansion of output on this scale have such adverse effects on the environment as to threaten a breakdown in the conditions under which human life can flourish? This, at any rate, is the threat of which environmentalists have warned us.

(a) The dangers of pollution

There is no doubt that heedless growth of output and reckless exploitation of natural resources can cause serious problems of pollution. We have plenty of examples in all the industrial countries, of the despoiling of the landscape by mineral workings and slagheaps, the pollution of the atmosphere by smoke and chemical fumes from factories, the pollution of watercourses by industrial domestic waste effluents. Agricultural developments can have similar results, with chemical fertilizers and pesticides such as DDT causing a run off which contaminates rivers and streams, of the ploughing up of virgin prairies and the cutting down of forests leading to erosion of fertile land and the creation of deserts and dustbowls.

With the intensification of the pace of development and the rapid application of new technologies, there have been fears of more serious results, because of the lack of adequate knowledge of side effects. Some of this we already experience. For instance, the motor car is a boon to its possessors since it provides a personal mobility of a convenience and flexibility which no previous form of transport could give. But when its use becomes general it involves all sorts of social costs such as noise and fumes and congestion. Under certain climatic conditions, as in Los Angeles or Tokyo, its multiplication can cause unpleasant and dangerous smog. Its exhaust fumes can be a serious source of lead poisoning. If everyone tries to use it at the same time and place we get the ultimate frustration of rush hour traffic jams in cities, or bank holiday crawls on the roads to the coast. If we try to get round this by building more roads, this is immensely costly in terms of the use of scarce land, labour and capital. If we go in for urban motorways we can end up by destroying the city itself beneath a maze of multi-carriageways, flyovers and parking spaces.

The development of aircraft has had similar effects. The aeroplane has done more to make us one world than the steamship and railways ever did. But the cost has been high in terms of vast and expensive airport facilities and the hardship caused to residents for miles around from the noise of aircraft landing and taking off.

There are plenty of other examples of pollution apparently getting out of hand. Pollution of waterways has in some cases gone so far as to threaten the regenerative capabilities of quite large enclosed spaces of water, such as Lake Erie in North America or Lake Baikal in Siberia. There have even been fears for some landlocked seas like the Baltic and the Mediterranean. The discharge toxic of effluents has given rise to fears of poisoning of fish and birds and through them of other animals which prey on them and eventually of man himself. The case of the Japanese villagers poisoned through eating fish contaminated by mercury in sea water caused widespread alarm.

More dramatic fears have been expressed for the future. For instance, the increased use of energy in industry might produce a rise in atmospheric temperature enough to cause melting of the Polar icecaps, with widespread flooding from rise in sea levels, and unknown effect on world climatic patterns. The widespread cutting down of forests in areas like the Amazon basin could affect the ability of plant life adequately to convert carbon dioxide into the oxygen on which animal and human life depends. Supersonic flight in the upper atmosphere could disrupt the layer of ozone which protects the earth from adverse radiation effects. The development of nuclear power as a replacement for oil and coal gives rise to serious dangers from possible leaks of radio-active material from power stations and even more serious problems of the safe disposal of waste which remains radio-active for centuries.[12]

These dangers arise out of the conflict mentioned above between private and social costs and benefits. Those who carry out development, whether they are private business men or public agencies, tend to take account of only those costs which fall on them in cash form. The atmosphere and the watercourses, into which effluents are disposed of, have been treated as free goods for which no price has to be paid, and hence the cost to the community of their pollution has not come into the reckoning. The same applies to the amenity of the surroundings, which can be destroyed by noise and by the unsightly appearance of the plant. The community needs to devise means of more effectively setting these costs against the benefits of greater material output, and of ensuring that some of the product is used to counteract pollution. This applies not only to actual pollution, but also to potential pollution which may arise from unexpected byproducts of new technical developments. Part of the social cost of these is the need for vigilance and for research into possible adverse effects on the world's living space. How successful have we been in doing all this and what are the prospects for the future?

(b) The prospects of counteracting pollution

In the developed industrial countries the prospects have considerably improved in recent years. Awareness of the dangers of pollution is now much greater, as is willingness to counteract it by public action.

Most countries in Western Europe and North America are now putting into operation policies to prevent pollution of the atmosphere and watercourses. In Japan, where very rapid industrial growth over the last twenty years has led to very serious problems, public opinion is now forcing similar action, and the same applies to the Soviet Union. In Britain there have been dramatic reductions in pollution of the air through stricter control over industrial emissions and restriction of the burning of coal in domestic grates. The heavy smogs which used to be a regular feature of our large cities are now mainly a thing of the past. A beginning has also been made in cleaning up our badly contaminated rivers, and fish are now reappearing in the Thames at London. In the United States, where concern has been especially vocal, stringent controls are also being introduced over the quality of emissions by motor vehicles.

Nor need the process of abatement be very costly. For the United States, which has the most elaborate programme, it has been estimated that the annual cost of the additional abatement measures now being undertaken is likely to be less than 1% of the gross national product, and the cumulative cost will be about 5% of the cumulative total of extra national output likely to be produced over the period 1972–76.[13] A study by the Organization for Economic Co-operation and Development, covering Western Europe, North America and Japan, suggests that the cost of reducing air pollution levels to their 1968 figure by 1980 would be only about 0·2 to 0·3% of the national product of the countries concerned.[14] Against this must be set very considerable benefits in improved health and amenity, as well as more tangible savings in laundry, cleaning of buildings, avoidance of corrosion and the like.

There is little doubt that in the developed countries it is possible not only to prevent a further spread of pollution, but to overcome a good deal of the damage of the past, at a very small cost in terms of use of the national product. This can be secured provided the public is aware of the dangers and opportunities and willing to accept appropriate policies to ensure that public interests prevail over immediate private interests. There must be an awareness not only of present dangers but of the potential future dangers from new developments of technology. Risks may have to be taken; for instance, should Concorde be allowed to fly, and should we further expand our nuclear power programme? But they should be taken responsibly, with the most careful possible weighing up of potential benefits against potential risks. At the same time, a rising real national product made possible by advancing technology makes it easier for us to spare the resources necessary to combat pollution. If we are getting better off, we can spend more on cleaning up rivers, introducing smoke control and renovating derelict areas without having to sacrifice other things, such as better living standards for the poor.

The situation in the developing world is much less favourable. It is here that the big increases in pollution are coming at the moment, as industrialization spreads over the countryside, slums grow up round the towns, effluents and sewage pour into the rivers and estuaries, and smoke and fumes belch into the atmosphere. Cutting down tropical forests and cultivation of lands of marginal rainfall brings dangers of erosion, while the need to get greater output from the land encourages unrestrained use of fertilizers and pesticides.

The governments and people of the developing countries are often impatient of protests by Western environmentalists. They are anxious to get the fruits of faster growth as the only means of breaking out of the vicious circle of poverty. They accuse the West of using concern for the environment as an excuse for stopping them from developing in order to keep them in neo-colonialist subordination. Poor countries are apt to regard the prospect of more goods and services as worth having, even if it involves the social cost of more pollution. They could not afford the means to carry out clean air and clean water measures by government action, and in many cases their governments are too weak, and too much under the control of industrial influences to be politically able to do so.

It is in Bombay and Calcutta, in São Paulo and Rio de Janeiro and the Amazon Basin, in Nairobi and Lagos and their like, that the big dangers to the environment are likely to arise in the near future. The immediate answer must come in part through the development of appropriate methods of intermediate technology, which have smaller and more easily controlled effects on the environment, and in part through greater help by the rich countries to the poor countries to enable them to introduce anti-pollution measures. In the long run only growth of real output can give the margin that will enable them to raise living standards and afford effectively to protect the environment.

(c) Conclusions on pollution

Our general conclusion must then be that while growth involves dangers to the environment, it also provides the means of counteracting these dangers. The important thing is to take a wide enough view of growth, to consider it in terms of a growth of total social welfare, and not merely in the flow of material goods and services. A clean atmosphere and pure rivers, pleasant amenities and towns which are healthy and beautiful and as free as possible from traffic noise and congestion, these are just as much part of a growth of real welfare as more motor cars and television sets or even freedom from dire want for the poor. The same applies to the assurance that technical progress is being used to make the environment more healthful to all, and does not harbour hidden menaces to the biosphere on which we all depend. An alert and vigorous public opinion, a willingness to spend on anti-pollution measures and a willingness to accept restrictions on our individual rights, to use our cars where and when we please, for instance, these are part of the price of achieving this.

7. *Is growth desirable?*

(a) The criticisms of feasibility have been much exaggerated

Recent attacks on the feasibility of growth can be seen to have been much exaggerated. We should be able to feed the prospectively growing world population, if we use all our knowledge and skills aright, though it will be a near run thing for the next few years. Resource supply is a much more complex matter than merely projecting cumulative increases of demand against known supplies, and given the various feedback effects, limited natural resources are not likely to be a serious obstacle within any practicable time scale. Pollution and the prospects of breakdown of the environment are a more real danger, but one that can be avoided if we are alert to it and willing to adapt our technological methods to overcome it, while growth itself gives us the means out of which to do this.

Growth is in fact largely a matter of good stewardship of the world's resources. It is a matter of using human skills, knowledge and experience, together with the natural resources of minerals, vegetables, animals and climatic conditions, so as to get a bigger output of the means of meeting human wants out of a given input of means of production. By doing this, we get a more effective material basis for men and women to have a better life, to be adequately fed, clothed and housed, to be freed from the grinding struggle for survival, to have a margin for developing their higher interests.

(b) Desirability of the methods of obtaining growth or of the use made of the product

Criticism of the desirability of doing this arises both from the methods by which it is achieved and from the use which is made of the increased product. In our Western market economy, the motive power for achieving growth is the striving for profit by business enterprises. Under conditions of modern large-scale industry this does not necessarily lead to the most efficient use of resources, as we shall see in the next chapter. Frequently, it leads to competitive innovation, with firms devising new products which only appear to be different and then seeking to create markets for them by large-scale advertising. Thus people are induced to want an ever greater variety of soaps and detergents, cosmetics, household gadgets, clothes, chocolates, cigarettes, drinks and so on, and often to discard their old and perfectly good car or washing machine for a new one with the latest gimmicks attached. Hence there is much restless striving for new things and new experiences which, it is held, cannot bring true satisfaction. Market conditions also lead to competition by firms to get and keep the best men, and hence to all the insecurity and need to get on associated with the rat race.

As a result of all this, the increase of product is not necessarily that which best meets human wants, but rather what the public can be induced to buy. Also it is very unevenly distributed, with poverty and lack of opportunity persisting within the developed countries getting little share in the increase.

In so far as all this is true, and there is a lot of truth in it, it points to the limitations of the free market as a method of meeting human wants. We need to develop more effective ways of exercising public control over the economy. In the mixed economies of the West, we have gone a long way in this direction already, with the Welfare State and the acceptance by governments of responsibility for controlling the general level and direction of economic activity. We have to devise means of enabling the community to use its economic system to achieve the social aims which are accepted as desirable, without sacrificing the flexibility of the market and the safeguards which it provides for individual freedom. After all, who is to decide what wants consumers 'ought' to satisfy, if we do not accept that they should decide for themselves how to spend their incomes between the goods and services available to them? Who are we to judge that they should not have the new car, or the new brand of cigarettes, or the new miracle detergent or glamorous cosmetic? Would we get better results with a centrally planned economy in which the government decided what people 'ought' to consume and provided only what they felt could be afforded?

This comes back to the question of motives, which we have already discussed several times and will have to look at more fully later. How far can the motive of self-interest, the drive for profits by firms, the drive for higher pay by individuals, the drive to get a higher standard of living for one's family, be so channelled as to achieve the greatest good of the greatest number? How far can it be replaced by a drive to secure the greatest welfare of the whole community, both within the country and on a world-wide basis?

The criticism of growth is thus that it results in inducing greed and self-seeking, rather than contentment and fulfilment and concern for the welfare of others. People are led to strive for more and more things, to become dissatisfied, to become jealous of those who are better off, to seek all the time for more money for themselves so that they can keep up with the Jones's, or keep ahead of the Smiths. But it is less clear that we can think of an alternative way of getting an efficient use of the world's resources which does not involve even greater disadvantages. Communist regimes can call forth great dedication and great self-discipline from their citizens, and can devote most of the resources of their communities to deliberately planned priorities. But they can only do this at the expense of extremely complex, rigid and fallible planning procedures, and at the cost of a degree of regimentation and ideological compulsion which destroys the freedom of individuals and families to 'do their own thing'.

What we have to decide is whether the benefits of growth in terms of a greater flow of material goods and services outweigh these disadvantages. Ultimately, growth gives us the means to make a better world, but it is up to us to decide how we are going to use these means. It is at this point that we can very appropriately turn to Christian beliefs about the meaning of life and what is good and worth while to see how they can help us in this choice.

8. *What light can be thrown on the problem by the Christian understanding?*

(*a*) *Growth is good, but it is not an end in itself*

Growth, like any other economic or political aim, cannot be regarded as an end in itself. It is a means of giving us greater resources which can be used in ways which promote God's glory and men's good, or the contrary.

There is plenty of evidence in the New Testament of the potential dangers of increasing wealth. We have already mentioned Christ's warnings that those who trust in riches find it hard to enter the kingdom (Mark 10.23–25; Matt. 19.23–24; Luke 18.24–25), and we can note also the parable of the Rich Man and Lazarus (Luke 16.19–31), and the warning that the love of money is the root of all evil (1 Tim. 6.10). There is also the story of the rich man who built large barns to store all his goods, oblivious of his imminent death (Luke 12.16–21). But in all these passages the emphasis is on the attitude to material goods, not on material goods themselves. It is hard for a rich man to enter the kingdom because he gets more concerned about keeping and extending his riches than about loving God and his neighbour. Jesus' remarks arose out of the case of the rich young man who went away sorrowful rather than accept his challenge to sell all he had and follow him. Riches can be a barrier that cuts us off from real contact with others and real concern and care for them, as in the case of Dives in the parable who was oblivious of the fate of Lazarus at his gate. The other rich man who built larger barns had built his security on material goods and had forgotten that the only true security is in love of God and trust in him. The love of money is the root of all evil because it leads men into many foolish and hurtful lusts and causes them to pierce themselves through with many sorrows. They become greedy and grasping and unscrupulous, suspicious and fearful of the designs of others on their money, or else they try to buy men's friendship and service. It is very difficult, though not impossible, to combine the pursuit of riches as a dominant aim in one's life, with the active pursuit of the knowledge of God and the service of others for his sake.

Yet there is also evidence to be found that it is in line with God's purposes that men should enjoy the good things of this world, receiving them as his gifts and using them to his glory. In the creation myth in Genesis, which embodies Old Testament thinking about the nature and purpose of the world, God is shown as looking on all he had made and finding it to be very good. He bids men to be fruitful and multiply and replenish the earth and have dominion over all the lower orders of creation (Gen. 1.26–31). The creation and all its resources are portrayed as essentially good, and it is only the perversion of the human will as depicted in the story of the Fall which leads to strife and hardship and injustice and exploitation.

Again, Christ tells us not to be anxious in seeking for food or clothes because our heavenly Father knows that we need these things, but to seek first the kingdom of God and his righteousness and all these things will be added to us (Matt. 6.31–33). And Paul urged the members of the early churches to work conscientiously to get their livings so that they might have the means to give to others (Eph. 4.28; II Thess. 3.10–12).

We can fairly conclude that it is in accordance with God's will that all his children should have the opportunity to enjoy to the full the good things which his world can provide. They should be freed from the grinding poverty and insecurity which makes a full and rich life so difficult for so many of them. And this can only be achieved for most of the world's people if there is both a steady growth in the size of the world's real product, and a more equitable distribution of it.

Moreover, the proper stewardship of men's talents and the world's natural resources involves using them so as to satisfy wants more effectively. True economic growth, of a kind which takes account of social benefits and social costs as well as purely private ones, can be held to be an expression of true stewardship. Remember Christ's parable of the talents, in which the servant who used his five talents to make five more, and the one who used his two talents to make two more, are commended, whereas the man who wrapped his one talent up in a napkin and buried it safely is condemned (Matt. 25.14–30). We would accept that this story is not primarily about money making, but about the responsible use of all one's gifts and opportunities – of one's talents in the modern figurative sense. Yet surely we can see here a relevance for wise stewardship by mankind of material gifts and human skills. We are to use them so as to get the most out of them in a world where resources are scarce relative to needs, not to squander or waste them or leave them idle because we do not know how to organize our economic systems properly.

Material things are good in themselves and they are to be enjoyed as God's gifts. It is by how we receive and use these gifts that we shall be judged.

(b) The dangers of hypocrisy

We must also beware of the dangers of hypocrisy in our attitude to the struggle of our brothers for a better standard of living. It is not for us to condemn others for not being satisfied with their present means and to talk about the blessings of poverty, while ourselves continuing to enjoy a comfortable middle-class way of life. There is often a good deal of this in the attitude of middle-class people to the efforts of trade unions to secure higher wages, or to the unwillingness of others to work regularly and consistently at hard, boring and unrewarding jobs. It is right to point out the inflationary effects of the wage-price spiral, or the effects of demarcation and restrictive practices on business costs, so long as we are prepared to question our own position in these matters also. Many traditionally better paid professional workers became militant in 1974–75, when they felt their real incomes slipping back in face of 20% inflation, or saw others who had previously been less well-paid overtaking them. Professional workers are not without their restrictive practices also, though they are usually advocated in terms of the need to preserve professional standards against less well-qualified auxiliaries.

Similarly, in our concern for the environment, we must take care that we are not primarily protecting our own pleasant amenities against those who in the past could not afford to share them. Some of the concern about the general ownership of motor cars arises from the fact that this may mean that formerly quiet parts of the countryside or coast which the better off could enjoy are now accessible to crowds of less acceptable visitors. There is also frequently violent opposition by inhabitants of middle-class residential areas against the advent of a council estate, or of a home for delinquents or alcoholics or the mentally handicapped. Again, the loss of amenity involved may be real and must be considered but the welfare of others in need must be weighed against it.

(c) The question of motives

Christians should also have a contribution to make towards resolving the conflict between the desirability of growth, as a means of more effectively meeting human wants, and the undesirable results of its pursuit, in the promotion of greed and envy and a desire for more and more things.

As we shall see more fully in the next chapter, the pursuit of gain has two aspects, as a motive to enterprise and work, and as a criterion by which to judge whether resources are being efficiently used. It is on the first aspect that Christians should have something useful to say. A motive is needed which is strong enough to induce devoted, sustained and conscientious work, which is wide enough to transcend the immediate interests of the worker in material gain, and which is flexible and imaginative enough to take in all the complications of doing justice to the different groups involved in the productive process.

Others have been more effective than Christians in harnessing an altruistic ideology to the cause of material advance. Notably the Communists have been able to make good use of this in Russia and more recently in China and Cuba. But the Communist ideology makes up for what it gains in intensity and drive by falling short in flexibility and compassion and has come to be too much embodied in an authoritarian political structure.

Christians should be able to see their work in terms of service to their fellows, a way of loving their neighbours which is part of their love of God. This gives a very strong incentive, but one in which freedom and responsibility are stressed. Service is not given out of blind obedience to a party line, but through a careful and responsible thinking out of how the work can best be done in the true best interests of all affected by it, consumers, colleagues, the general public, those in other countries. This is a difficult and demanding responsibility and one which Christians so far have done little to fulfil, but it points a way forward. Groups of Christians should be discussing the implications of it for their own jobs together with their colleagues who do not share their commitment.

The same attitude applies to our responsibility as citizens for the welfare of our fellows at home and abroad, as expressed through the activities of our government. The paying of taxes, the casting of our vote, the playing of our part in the forming of responsible public opinion, the use we make of the public services, all demand the same kind of thoughtful commitment.

The other side of this shows up in the use which we make ourselves of the national product. Our motive for wanting a responsibly achieved growth of output should not be primarily so that our living standard may rise. Hence we must give more thought to the type of simple, yet thankful and joyful, use of God's good gifts which is appropriate. In our modern urban society we cannot realistically live in actual poverty, but we certainly should not be living in conspicuous consumption, and we need also to be generous and disciplined in our use of money to support good causes, both by personal giving and through our payment of taxes. Being content with the old car or the old television or washing machine, not seeking for a lavish and luxurious house nor for extravagant holidays, can be an important piece of Christian witness. But it must be done naturally and spontaneously and joyfully and not be allowed to degenerate into rigoristic legalism. Nor must it be accompanied by censoriousness of others who for various reasons take a different line.

(*d*) *True stewardship*

We have seen that the question of growth is really one of stewardship. Stewardship means making efficient and not wasteful use of resources and that will normally mean getting a bigger output for a given input. Christians can therefore give a lead in working out what it means in particular economic situations.

Thus it is good stewardship to use improved techniques so as to get more finished steel or copper out of a given tonnage of ore and fuel. It is good stewardship when rising prices of materials force us to recycle more of them. It is good stewardship to go in for managed cropping and replanting of forests, rather than cutting them down and leaving them to waste. It is good stewardship to plough and crop the land so that its fertility is not lost through erosion, and to take care that the harvest is not ruined through rats, insects or exposure to the weather. It is good stewardship to enable men and women to do the kind of work which makes the best use of their talents and in return to get a fair share of the product, rather than exhausting them through drudgery, or keeping them doing repetitive jobs which underuse their gifts, or leaving them idle without work.

It is also good stewardship to take care that in our agriculture, mining and manufacturing we do as little as possible to despoil the environment through laying the land waste, or polluting the air and the water with our effluents. Christian thinking can help here, too, by bringing to bear a certain reverence for the creation as God's gift. Man as the crown of the creation has the right to replenish the earth and subdue it, but he is to use it as God's gift, and that implies a concern for the ecological balance between climate, materials, plants and animals. As against systems of belief which make man the measure and centre of all things, this Christian emphasis introduces a certain healthy restraining influence, provided we can think out realistically and not merely sentimentally what its implications are for practical policies.

But the consideration of growth and its advantages and costs, its opportunities and responsibilities has raised many issues with deeper implications for the whole process by which we get our living. It is time, therefore, to turn to a more systematic exploration of these in the next chapter.

7

Economic Organization and Participation

1. *Introduction*

We have now considered in fair detail some of the most important economic issues affecting the world today. We have looked at inflation, at poverty and inequality within the rich countries, at the gulf between rich and poor in the world as a whole, and at the question of economic growth and its relation to pollution. All of these studies have forced on our attention fundamental questions about the way in which the economy is organized, the problems inherent in its working, and the motive power which drives it.

We begin our investigation of these by looking at the basic economic functions which have to be carried out in any system. We go on to discuss the two main principles of organization, the market and command principles, and the various combinations between them to be found in actual economies today of the West and the East. Then we look at various alternatives that have been tried or proposed. This leads on to a summarizing of the underlying problems, both technical and human, which have to be solved if a satisfactory economic system is to be devised, and we end once again by looking at the kinds of insights which the Christian faith can give us towards solving them.

2. *The basic economic functions*

An economic system is a means by which we organize resources, human skills, natural materials and manufactured capital goods, in order to produce products to satisfy human wants. This process can be broken down into a number of basic functions, which have to be carried out by any such system.[1] They are as follows:

(a) The demand problem

The first problem is how we decide which human wants will be met, what kinds of goods and services will be produced and in what quantities and qualities. Human wants are infinite; there is no limit to what demands could be met, if we had the resources, but productive means are limited. Therefore there has to be a choice. More clothes may mean less food, more meat less bread, more television sets less guns and tanks, more cars less houses, more houses less schools. More teachers may mean fewer civil servants or social workers, and so on. The fundamental economic truth is that if you use resources for one purpose, you cannot use them for something else.

(b) The production problem

The second problem is how to combine productive resources in order to make available the goods and services which it is decided to produce, how much labour to use, of what level of skill, what kind of machines, what kind of raw materials, whether to use more labour-intensive or more capital-intensive methods. These two questions are obviously interdependent, because what wants are in fact met and what goods are produced depends greatly on the production methods chosen. A technical innovation, like the development of the internal combustion engine, or the electronics of television, makes it possible for a whole new range of demands to be met, for personal transport by car or goods transport by lorry, or home entertainment from the 'box'. Very often, what can be produced, and how cheaply relative to other goods, determines the pattern of what is demanded. Yet logically demand is prior, for the economy exists to meet people's wants.

(c) The exchange and distribution problem

The third problem is how to share out the product among the population, both those who take part in its production and those who cannot do so. This has two interrelated aspects, that of the mechanics of distribution, that is the means which are used to give people an entitlement to share in the product, and that of the proportions in which different people are entitled to various sized shares of the product. In other words, are goods and services sold for a price, or distributed by some sort of direct rationing, and does income depend entirely upon the value of one's contribution of labour or capital, or is some part of it at least distributed as of right, as we do with basic social services like education and medical treatment? The solution adopted to these problems in turn reacts back on demand and production, because the distribution of effective consumption power greatly affects the types of goods demanded, and also affects the willingness of income receivers to offer the services of their labour or capital for production.

(d) The saving and investment problem

The fourth problem is how to divide the product of the economy between current use and future use. How much of it should be used up by the present consumption of goods and services of all kinds to satisfy wants? How much should be withdrawn from current consumption through saving and used for investment to maintain and improve productive facilities, so that we can not only continue to produce in the future, but also enjoy the benefit of more efficient methods and more varied products? This decision in turn reacts back on the others, affecting income distribution, the supply of factors and the types and quantities of goods demanded.

3. *The market and command principles*

Actual economies are all exceedingly complex and varied. Small-scale private producers, large-scale companies, publicly owned enterprises and the government itself all take different roles in different cases. Nevertheless, two clear principles can be distinguished, which they all embody in varying degrees, the market principle and the command principle.

(a) The market principle

The market principle implies an economy organized on the basis of independent producing and consuming units, which buy and sell goods and services between one another in return for prices. There are markets both for products, that is goods and services produced by business firms and bought by households to satisfy their wants, and for factors of production, such as labour, men and women selling their skills to firms in return for wages and salaries, or capital, such as machines and tools, raw materials and partly finished products, or for land, for farms, houses, factories and other uses.

In a market system the decision what to produce depends on households and individuals deciding how to spend their incomes, for what they want to buy will sell well and be profitable to produce, and what they do not want will sell badly and will result in losses to the producers.

The decision how to produce depends on the choices of business firms, who will hire labour and buy plant and machinery and raw materials and combine them in the way which enables them to produce most profitably. How the product is distributed depends on the levels of incomes received by those who sell the services of labour, capital or land to the producers, and on the relative prices at which different goods and services sell. The division as between present and future production depends on decisions by households as to how much to save out of income and of firms as to how much to save out of profits, and on decisions by firms on how much to invest in plant, equipment and stocks. These are affected in turn by the prevailing rates of interest and availability of credit in the financial markets.

Thus the regulating mechanisms in a market economy, which are relied upon to secure the efficient use of resources, are the price system, competition, and the motives of seeking satisfaction and profit. If too much is being supplied in any market, and not enough demanded, prices will tend to go down, thus discouraging production and encouraging consumption. If too little is being supplied, and too much demanded, prices will tend to go up, discouraging consumption and encouraging production. Consumers balance their purchases of different goods in terms of their relative prices, so as to divide their incomes between them in the way which gives them the greatest satisfaction. Producers balance their production of different types of goods, and the proportions of different types of labour and capital which they use to make them, in accordance with the prices at which they can sell the various products and the volumes they can sell at each price, and the prices they have to pay for factors, so as to maximize profits.[2] Competition between different producers supplying the same market and different consumers buying in it is relied upon to ensure that neither can exploit the other and each must respond to price changes.

Advantages of the market system can be summarized as follows:

It is automatic. It does not require any overall decisions as to what goods and services to produce, or what quantities of labour, materials and plant to use in producing them. It relies on the interaction of the decisions of large numbers of independent consumers and producers each following their own judgment of their own best interests.

It is self-regulating. There is automatic feedback through the price system if too much is produced of any one thing and not enough of another, or if too many people are seeking to be employed in one job and not enough in another. A fall in prices in the case of overproduction, or a rise in the case of underproduction signals back from the retailers through the wholesalers to the manufacturers and induces corrective action.

It is flexible. There is always scope for new producers to develop new types of product or process and test out the results in the market. If they meet a need they will prosper. On the other hand, obsolete types of production are discouraged by falling sales and falling profits.

It encourages political and social freedom. There is always scope for those whose views are unpopular, or who want to do their own thing, to support themselves by their own efforts, or to find a congenial employer. No one is dependent for his livelihood on a single, monolithic state, and if he offends one employer, he can move to another.

Many of the disadvantages we have met already in discussing the various ways in which the government has increasingly intervened in the economies of the West. We can summarize them as follows:

There is an imbalance between producers and consumers. This has become more prominent with the growing importance of large-scale technology. Although many small firms still exist and flourish, modern economies are increasingly dominated by large-scale firms for which the unorganized consumers are no match in bargaining power. In these conditions, firms tend to compete by developing new varieties of product and then creating a market for them by large-scale branding and advertising. Competition between producers cannot be relied upon to ensure that firms always produce efficiently and give the consumers what will most guarantee their satisfaction.[3]

It is unable to take account of social costs and benefits. As we saw in chapter 6, the market system, being based on prices, takes account only of private costs and benefits, those which enter into the money costs borne by producers and the money prices paid by consumers. It cannot take account of social costs and benefits which are not reflected in prices, such as pollution and traffic congestion, or the benefits to the community as a whole from such services as education and medical treatment, or public transport.

Carrying this a stage further, the market cannot be used for the supply of public goods, those goods and services whose benefit is wholly or mainly social, not private. If these are provided at all, everyone gets the benefit from them, so that no one is willing to pay an adequate price for them. Such goods as defence, law and order, town and country planning, roads, sewerage and refuse disposal must in varying degrees be provided by the government and paid for out of taxation.

It is unequal. The market system distributes income in accordance with the market price placed on the services of the labour, capital or land supplied by the recipients, and this leads, as we saw in chapter 4, to a very unequal distribution of incomes and opportunities.

It is unstable. Left to itself, the market system does not produce a steady rate of growth of output, as technological progress proceeds, but rather a tendency to violent fluctuations of expansion and contraction, boom and slump. The reasons for this are complex, but are bound up with the nature of the investment process. Firms have to decide how much to invest in new productive capacity on the basis of what they expect the market for their products to be several years hence, when the new plant comes into operation. During periods of prosperity, there is a tendency for expectations to be excessive, so that too much is produced and the expected profits are not made. When this happens, output and investment are cut back and this leads to a slump. The upward and downward fluctuations are intensified by the multiplier process described in chapter 3, section 1 (a) above.

Finally, the market system is *not capable of concerted quick action in a crisis*. For this reason, it tends to be superseded during major wars, when government action through controls and rationing can divert resources more directly to war purposes. Similarly, if a country wishes to carry out a quick programme of development of basic industries, as Russia did in the 1930s, or China today, a command system is more effective.

(*b*) *The command principle*

The command principle implies a system in which all the various economic decisions are taken deliberately and consistently by a centralized body of planners, who give instructions to the various enterprises to be carried out. Thus the planners decide what goods and services should be produced, and in what quantities and qualities. They decide how resources should be used to produce them, how much of each kind of labour, each kind of plant, each kind of material. If the principle were fully applied, they would also decide how the product was allocated among consumers, by some sort of rationing system, and what kind of work everyone should do. Because of the rigidity which this involves, this is not usually done, except in emergency situations. The planners do, however, seek to prescribe what price should be charged for each type of goods and service, and what rate of wage or salary should be paid for each job. The planners also decide how the product shall be divided between current and future consumption, for they draw up investment plans and deliberately divert resources to carry them out, thus forcing the community to save by reducing the flow of consumer goods available.

The regulating principle is thus deliberate decision by the planners, and the explicit balancing of expected flows of resources of all kinds between different uses, and not response by consumers and producers to market prices.

The command system has certain advantages.

The priorities of the government can be directly and deliberately carried out. If it is decided to build up heavy industries, like coal and steel and electric power, or to reorganize the structure and methods of agriculture, in principle at least the government can go ahead and do this. The planners can decide how many tons of coal or steel are to be produced, or how many units of power, and can carry out the necessary investment in plant to bring this about. Detailed production targets are given to the State enterprises in each industry, and they are required to carry them out.

Similarly, *social priorities can be met directly*, and those types of production deemed to have social benefits can be expanded, and those involving social costs contracted, deliberately, without having to bother about the costs or the profits of private producers. Income inequality can be reduced to the extent considered desirable by the planners, for rates of pay are fixed by them and need not be related, in theory at least, to the supply of and demand for different kinds of skills.

The inbuilt instability of the market can also be avoided, and, again in principle at least, the economy can be planned to grow steadily at the rate considered practicable or desirable on the basis of available resources.

The disadvantages of the command system arise from the concentration of control which gives it these advantages, for this presumes a degree of knowledge, competence, farsightedness, intelligence and sheer hard work on the part of the planners, which is almost impossible to attain. Hence the main drawbacks are:

It is extremely complex. Deliberate decisions have to be taken as to the quantities and qualities to be produced of all the thousands, if not millions, of products which can be made, and as to the qualities and quantities of all the thousands of types of labour, materials and plants needed to make them. To reproduce the kind of network of relationships which the market system involves would mean solving millions of simultaneous equations. This is possible perhaps with computers, but interpreting the results puts an impossible burden on the human beings who have to take the decisions. In practice, only broad categories of products and factors are planned for, but even so the complexity is great enough.

It is vulnerable to failures. If the output of any one of these goods fails to reach the planned level, this is liable to throw the whole system out of balance. Thus bad weather may upset the corn harvest or disease kill off the cattle, or floods or snow interrupt the transport of coal, or drought cut hydro-electric power supply. Or the miners may fail to produce their quotas, because these have been fixed too high. This may reduce steel production, which in turn cuts the supply of machines for industry, and the whole programme is thrown out. Or production may be upset because not enough skilled workers can be found to man the machines. And there are innumerable other possibilities of disruption.

The effect of this is made worse because, with fixed prices, *there is no automatic feedback* if the supply of any goods does not match the demand. If too much is produced, it piles up unsold; if too little, there are shortages and queues. But these are not reflected in price changes and hence are not transmitted back to the manufacturers, who have their fixed quota of goods to produce.

It is inflexible. Any change in the production quotas, or in the quantities of factors to be used, or in prices, can only be made by deliberate action by the planners. This is inevitably delayed by lack of information and hence often comes too late, so that it can make a situation worse rather than better.

Incentives and criteria are also a serious problem. Managers of enterprises are instructed to produce specified quantities of output, using specified inputs of factors, but it is difficult to make sure that they do so in ways which lead to efficiency. There are well-known stories of how, if the target is specified in terms of the number of units of, say, shirts, quality will be scamped to ensure quantity; if in terms of weight, e.g. tons of steel, there will be an incentive to make heavy goods instead of light ones. Specifications have to be made ever more detailed to counteract this, and policing becomes ever more difficult. In the absence of profits, there is no direct incentive to plan fulfilment, and complicated systems of bonuses for success and penalties for failure have to be devised.

Finally, *dangers to political freedom* arise from the highly centralized and monolithic structure of a command economy. Political power and economic power are concentrated in the same hands, and the scope for nonconformity and independence of views is much reduced, if dissidents are dependent on the State for their livelihood.

(c) Control and ownership

Although the distinction between the market and command principles of organization is bound up with that between private and public ownership, the two are not the same.

In general, economies which are mainly market-based are also based primarily on private ownership by individuals and companies, whereas economies based on the command principle are characterized mainly by public ownership through State enterprises. This is not necessarily true, however. There have been theoretical models of economies with public ownership in which enterprises are instructed to operate in a free market, responding to prices and seeking to achieve the most efficient output in terms of some prescribed general criterion.[4] The Yugoslav system of co-operative enterprises operating independently within a very general overall plan is similar. On the other hand there have been economies where the command principle bulks large, but in general private ownership is retained. The corporate economies of Fascist Italy and Nazi Germany were of this type, and so very largely were the economies of the main belligerents during the Second World War.

This raises issues of what the relationship should be between ownership and control, which we discuss later in this chapter. In the modern market economy, ownership of joint stock companies remains nominally in the hands of the ordinary shareholders, but they exercise little control over them other than the negative one of selling their shares if they do not get an adequate return on them. Actual control is in the hands of salaried directors and top managers, who are effectively responsible to no one, though they are legally responsible only to the shareholders. Complicated issues arise as to how the interests of the employees, the consumers and the general public can best be safeguarded.

On the other hand, nationalized industries, though publicly owned, are expected to act as commercial undertakings within a framework of government policy intended to take account of the public interest. In practice it has proved very difficult to combine commercial freedom and public responsibility in their operations.

4. *Mixed economies*

All actual economies are in varying degrees mixtures of the market and command principles. The market economies of the West have a growing public sector in them, in the form both of direct government services and of nationalized and partly nationalized industries. They also operate within a framework of government controls and economic policies which becomes ever more widely embracing. The command economies of the East retain considerable market sectors, especially in agriculture and small crafts and services. They have also been experimenting with the reintroduction of market elements in order to give greater flexibility and better incentives.

There have also been a number of experiments and proposals arising out of dissatisfaction with the performance of existing economies both in the West and the East. Among them are the co-operative socialism of Yugoslavia, the charismatic populist socialism of China and Cuba, and the aspirations of the so-called 'New Left' towards a non-authoritarian socialism.

All these developments we must now look at.

(a) The mixed economies of the West

There is no doubt that the Western industrial economies are mixed. In Britain, for instance, government services in kind, such as defence, education, health services, roads and administration now make up nearly a fifth of the national product, while if transfers of income, like social security, and capital expenditure, are included, over half the national product passes through its hands. The public sector, including central and local government and the nationalized industries, accounts for about 40% of our total gross fixed capital investment each year and for about a quarter of our total occupied manpower. Figures for other countries of Western Europe are not very different from these, and though those for the United States and Japan are somewhat lower, the trend is in the same direction.

The growth in the role of the public sector takes a number of forms. There has been an extension of public services to meet social wants not met adequately through the market. This includes social services like social security, education, health and housing, as described in chapter 4, but also environmental services like cleansing, sewerage, parks and recreational provision, and anti-pollution measures, and economic services like roads, research and development and aid to industry. There has been an extension of public ownership of industry, in Britain mainly in the fields of public utilities such as transport and communications, power and water supply, but extending also to manufacturing industries like steel, and more recently to individual firms like Rolls Royce, and now to be extended more widely to industries such as shipbuilding and aircraft. In some countries public ownership of industry has been more widespread, as in France where it includes the main commercial banks and Renault motors, or in Italy, where the State holding companies IRI and ENI have a wide range of subsidiaries throughout the industrial and commercial fields.[5]

There has also been an attempt by the government to take a widening responsibility for controlling the general framework of economic conditions within which industry and commerce operate. This has included short-term stabilization, holding the balance between inflation and deflation by means of fiscal and monetary policy, which almost all governments now attempt to do, with varying success. It has included less successful attempts at long-term planning to secure a steady rate of growth, by co-operation between government and industry along the lines pioneered in France in the 1950s. Governments likewise pursue regional policies, using a mixture of incentives and deterrents to encourage industrial and commercial development in regions where basic industries are declining, and to restrain it in those where growth is too rapid. Another line has been the development of policies to try to counteract abuses of economic power by large firms or groups through monopolies and restrictive practices, and so encourage the promotion of efficiency through competition.

Now there are signs of the evolving of more active policies of direct co-operation between governments and industrial managements. Governments will supply capital to firms for investment, in return for a part share in their ownership and a say in their investment and employment policies. In Britain this process began with the Conservatives' Industry Act of 1972, under which, for instance, it is being applied to British Leyland. The Labour government intends to carry it further with its National Enterprise Board, which will have power to invest capital in companies and take shareholdings in them, and its proposals for planning agreements, by which firms will be invited to co-ordinate their investment plans with government policy.

In the earlier years of the post-1945 period it looked as if the mixed economy was successfully combining the merits of free enterprise and public control. The heavy unemployment of the 1930s and the successions of booms and slumps of the past had been largely overcome. Full employment prevailed with only slight departures from it during recessions. Growth of real incomes was fast and living standards were rising. The Welfare State seemed to be overcoming the worst problems of poverty and inequality (though not so successfully as appeared, as we saw in chapter 4).

More recently there has been some disillusionment with its achievements. The problem of inflation, which seemed a small price to pay for prosperity when it was only a few per cent a year, has now become much more serious and intractable. In the spring of 1975 it seemed to be threatening ever steeper rises in prices together with rising unemployment and continued industrial unrest.

With greater prosperity, aspirations have risen. Whereas in the late forties the ending of grinding poverty seemed to be a remarkable achievement, those who are less well off now want to share in the greater wealth which they see being enjoyed by the more fortunate. In Britain in particular there has been an aspiration for a rate of growth of real incomes which the relatively sluggish economy has not been able to provide. There has also been resentment at the still considerable inequalities of income and opportunities which seem to be inescapable.

There have been aspirations also towards a greater degree of participation in control over the conditions under which people get their livelihood. Men are increasingly unwilling to acquiesce in a situation in which they are liable to lose their jobs suddenly without prior consultation because a firm is being reorganized, or in which they are required to operate new types of plant and new working arrangements without their advice being sought. Nor are they prepared to take arbitrary orders from superiors. Most people's horizons are probably still fairly limited, and they would not want to share in active responsibility for the wider policies of their employers. Yet they want to be treated with the dignity of adult persons and to be consulted about matters on which their experience is relevant and in which their interests are directly involved.

These various malaises seem to be especially prevalent in Britain. We get the impression that the mixed economy is working more successfully, say, in West Germany, or France, or Sweden, or Japan, or even in the United States, than it is here.

The reasons for this are complex and have been the subject of much controversy in recent years, bound up as they are with the question of Britain's relatively slow rate of economic growth. Briefly, one can suggest the following.

Since large-scale industrialization came later in these countries than in Britain, their economies are more dynamic and more orientated towards rapid technical change and innovation. In the case of the Western European countries and also of Japan, a further impetus was given to this by the need to reconstruct industry after wartime devastation.

Although British basic technology is as good as any, British industry is less good at commercial innovation.

Some of our competitors, too, have been going through a later and more rapid social revolution, as a result of technical innovation. They have had large peasant populations which are displaced from the land by the rise of agricultural productivity and provide an abundant source of labour lacking to Britain. They have also had a larger proportion of small traders and independent craftsmen who are similarly displaced by technical revolutions in distribution and the service trades and can be absorbed into industry.

Britain is also suffering from her changed position in the world. Our economy depended more than most on the import of primary products from outside Europe, and the export of manufactures to the primary producing countries, as well as on large-scale investment in these countries, which flowed back in a demand for British machinery and plant. The recent rapid growth in world trade has been mainly in specialized manufactured products between the main industrial countries, and Britain has been less well-placed to take advantage of this than our competitors have been.

Because of our older history of development, many of our structures and attitudes tend to be set in older and less flexible ways. This is especially true of our system of industrial relations. Our trade union structure is very fragmented, with different unions having historical rights to organize different types of worker within most industries. Because of this, the full-time officers of the unions have limited powers, and the initiative has come to be taken largely by the semi-official shop stewards, who have to act as local leaders and bargainers in each workplace, but over whom the union leadership has little control. This makes orderly bargaining difficult, as compared with the centralized and more professionalized unions of West Germany, Scandinavia or the United States. Our managements, too, have tended to be more wedded to older ways and less professionalized than their competitors, and this applies both in industrial relations and in general production and commercial policy.

(b) The mixed economies of the East

The command economies of the East have also been moving towards modifying the command principles with certain elements of the market system. This has been more true in countries like Hungary, Poland and Czechoslovakia, which are very dependent on international trade with the West, than it has been of the much larger and more self-sufficient economy of the Soviet Union.

Even in Russia the command system never applied completely. Agriculture is mainly organized in collective farms, which are technically co-operatives, and which are free to sell their surplus produce over and above stipulated quotas on the free market. The peasants can also sell the produce of their private plots in the market, and this forms a significant part of the supply of vegetables, fruit, eggs and poultry. Independent craftsmen and professional workers are allowed to sell their services, provided they do not have employees. Private ownership of dwellings is also allowed and is the rule in the countryside. In most of the other East European countries the scope of the private sector is greater. The peasants usually own their own land, though they are often organized into co-operatives. There is more scope for small-scale private trading, though in all of them except Yugoslavia large-scale industry and commerce are in the hands of the State enterprises.

To get over the problems of the rigidity and complexity of planning decisions, the lack of feedback and the inadequacy of incentives and criteria, there have been experiments in giving enterprises more freedom to adapt to market conditions. Instead of being given fixed output targets and fixed input specifications, they are given profit targets and some scope to decide for themselves what output to produce and what labour and materials to use, within an overall plan. There has been considerable ideological conflict over how far this process should go. Marxist purists tend to denounce it as revisionism and a betrayal of the principle of the planned use of resources. Those countries which have to sell competitively in Western markets have been compelled to go further in this direction than the Soviet Union, which is both more insulated and more ideologically committed.

In no case other than Yugoslavia has the reintroduction of the market gone far enough to do more than modify a basically command structure. The aim is to maintain a centrally planned control over the use of resources, while mitigating its worst rigidities, and also to meet consumers' wants more effectively. As incomes begin to rise, the public becomes increasingly dissatisfied with the poor supplies of consumers' goods and services which the established system has provided. In countries like Poland, Hungary and Czechoslovakia, where Communism is an alien imposition rather than an indigenous growth, concessions have to be made to prevent public unrest. Russian influence and ideological commitment, however, prevent changes from going too far, as events in Czechoslovakia in 1968 made plain.

(c) Various experiments at third ways

Among the various experiments, both theoretical and practical, at ways alternative to the mainly market economies of the West and the highly centralized command economies of the Soviet bloc, we can mention the following:

After the break with Russia in the later forties, the Yugoslav economy was reorganized on a free market co-operative basis. Large-scale industrial and commercial enterprises became co-operatives, owned and controlled by those who worked in them. Considerable freedom was allowed for small-scale private enterprises in fields like distribution, catering and other services. In agriculture the peasants became independent and were only loosely organized into co-operatives. Enterprises were left almost entirely free to determine their own output, investment and prices in response to the market. Central planning was concerned only with the overall line of investment, mainly to ensure the more rapid development of the poorer regions in the south of the country. The immediate upshot of exposure to the market was many bankruptcies and much unemployment among over-expanded former State enterprises, but the system has been reasonably successful and has led to a fairly fast rate of growth in a largely underdeveloped economy. As in neighbouring Italy, however, there has been considerable polarization, with the more industrialized republics of Slovenia and Croatia going ahead faster than the poorer, less developed republics of the South.

Other socialist regimes have reacted against the rigid authoritarianism of the Soviet system in the opposite direction. In both China and Cuba the aim has been to preserve the spontaneous enthusiasm of the masses of the people and enlist it for the building up of the economy.

The essence of the Cultural Revolution in China was a determination by Mao Tse-tung and his followers to prevent the party bureaucrats and the technical experts obtaining the kind of entrenched privileged position which he felt that they had secured in Russia. The Chinese revolution, unlike the Russian, had been based on the peasants, and Mao was anxious also to avoid any split between urban and rural society, or workers and intellectuals. The establishment of rural communes, in which appropriate agricultural techniques can be applied as well as rural industries, seems to have been successful in bringing about a genuine revitalization of Chinese agriculture. The drift of population to the towns has been stopped. The sense of enthusiasm, and of all groups working together for the benefit of the community, seem to be genuine, in spite of the undoubted ideological conformity and political repression which they involve.

Similarly in Cuba a genuine revolution in the countryside has been achieved and a mobilizing of popular support. The aim is constantly to enlist the motive of working together to build a new community, rather than for personal gain. The cost, however, has been considerable: half a million refugees from among the old upper and middle classes, and a need for massive Russian aid to keep the balance of payments solvent.

Somewhat on the same lines, though less totalitarian in its methods, is the Tanzanian rural socialism inspired by President Nyerere. The aim here is to build the community through self-help on the basis of village co-operatives, using small-scale technology rather than relying on large-scale foreign investment and urbanization.

The disappointment with the achievements of the mixed economy in the West, and the reaction from the rigidities and ideological repression of Soviet style communism, have led to the rise of the phenomenon known as the 'New Left'. This represents renewed aspirations towards an ideal socialist society in which the original vision of Marx would be realized, of the State withering away and each being free to give according to his abilities and receive according to his needs. Politically, its exponents represent many strands, some Maoist, influenced by Chinese success in avoiding an authoritarian elite structure, some Trotskyist, thinking in terms of permanent revolution rather than Stalin's revolution in one country, some anarchist, and inclined to regard men as naturally good and only made corrupt by the coercive machinery of the State.

The vision of the New Left is in many ways attractive and contains an idealism which a cynical world badly needs. But it is fair to criticize them for naivety. Their immediate concerns are almost entirely political, and they tend to brush aside the obstinate problems of economics, such as how to produce enough goods and services to overcome the problem of poverty, how to harness the self-interest of men and turn it into constructive channels, how to combine the large-scale organization and planning needed for successful production with the freedom and participation needed for individual satisfaction – in fact, all the problems which both the market and the command systems have wrestled with.

In the political field also they are often naive in their trust in violence as the necessary method of destroying the present corrupt structures which bar the way to their ideal. While it is sometimes true that where an entrenched ruling economic and political system proves resistant to gradual peaceful change, a violent upheaval is the inevitable result, yet violence has a way of destroying the ideals for which it is espoused. The fears, the bitterness and the hostilities which it engenders are apt to lead to the setting up of regimes which owe their existence to repression and have to remain repressive. It is no coincidence that so many revolutions have been followed by authoritarian regimes, as in France, Russia, China, Spain, to name but a few countries.

5. *The underlying economic problems*

Our study of the two basic principles by which the choice between alternative uses of scarce resources can be organized has brought out a number of problems and difficulties which in fact have come out in all our discussion of particular economic problems up to this point. We now need to sum them up by bringing out the main underlying issues involved in them.

(*a*) *How to combine authority with participation and security*

In any organization there must be differences of function. Some have to take the lead in deciding what is to be done while others must accept instructions and carry them out. Yet, for success, all must feel that they have a responsible share in what is being done, that their skill and experience are being fully used, that they have some control over the work they do. An organization based on blind obedience, fear and coercion can never enlist wholehearted support, though it may achieve a certain efficiency in the short run.

So long as businesses are small, this does not cause great problems. The boss is near enough to his men to explain to them what he is doing and why, and they can know and trust him. The small-scale, privately owned business, though often very insecure, can still provide men and women with a way of life which they find rewarding.

But the techniques of modern production and administration make this difficult. Both in industry and commerce and in government and the public services, the economies of scale are now so decisive that enterprises and departments must typically be large. Overall policy cannot be decided by mass meetings, but must be worked out by those who have the expertise and experience to do so, for only they can take a wide enough view. The leaders of big business have to commit investments of millions of pounds on the basis of their understanding of trends in the national economy and world trade for several years ahead. On top of this they must make allowance for changing government policy.

Yet the rank and file are getting increasingly dissatisfied with a situation where they are expected to do what their bosses tell them, without regard for their interests and experience or their working conditions. Most people it is true are content to earn a reasonable living and leave management to the managers. Yet they want to be sure that management is not neglecting their interests, and many feel that they have something to contribute from their experience of their jobs. Above all they want security. They will not accept willingly a situation in which they are suddenly told that a drop in orders means that several thousands of them must be made redundant next week. Or that the machines on which they learnt their jobs and by which they get their livings are suddenly obsolete and must be scrapped.

Nevertheless, these situations arise. The bottom does drop out of markets, and machines do become obsolete. If firms are not flexible enough to meet these changes, they will go out of business. Or they may be kept going only by extremely wasteful subsidization of overmanning and unproductive methods. In the spring of 1975 this was being strikingly brought home to us in the cases of British Steel and British Leyland. Though no one wants to lose his job, it is not desirable in terms of efficient use of resources, nor good for self-respect, to keep people at work doing jobs that are not really needed.

We have to find means of combining participation with expert leadership, and security with flexibility. We are far from doing so yet, and we may expect to see many more experiments with works councils, shop and departmental councils, workers' representation on boards of directors, agreed procedures for consultation on reorganization, and the like.

(*b*) *How to combine job satisfaction with efficiency*

Related to the last issue is that of the nature of much of the world's work. It is probably true that for most men and women most of the time, daily work has been largely a matter of drudgery, of uninteresting and often arduous toil that must be got through in order to get a living. Only a minority have been able to have the kind of work which they find a joy to do. Middle-class professional people are among those most likely to do so, and even they know that the most interesting jobs have their drudgery element, like correcting examination papers for the teacher.

We can rejoice that one result of technological development is that the element of hard physical labour is increasingly being taken out of so much work, since machines can do it better. More recently, computers and other electronic devices are taking over much of the drudgery of routine clerical work also. On the whole, modern technology creates a wider range of more interesting and rewarding jobs for those who control it and make use of it. But it is not without its problems. There is much monotonous, repetitive work in modern industry, and sometimes it is also arduous, as in the motor industry where men have to keep up with the production line. Such work can give little inherent satisfaction, for those who do it see only their own tiny bit of the job. The only compensation for it can be in high earnings, or in the comradeship of the work group, which many find to be a source of satisfaction. At the same time, much of the old joy in skilled craftsmanship which the older system could bring to those fortunate to have a trade, has inevitably been swept away.

Many of the repetitive jobs in industry are being eliminated in turn by automation, with computers programmed to monitor the machines instead of human beings. But this carries further the process of polarization. Those without the ability or the education and training to become computer operators, technicians or administrators may find that the opportunities for unskilled workers are drying up. Already in the United States the high school drop-out finds it difficult to get a job of any sort.

Bearing in mind that the world's work must be done, and that there is likely always to be an element of drudgery in it, there is still a need to make jobs as interesting and rewarding as we can, so that those who do them feel they are making a worthwhile contribution and are not merely in it for the money. Already job enrichment has become a catch phrase. There are experiments in training people to do several jobs interchangeably, instead of just one. There are schemes for replacing production lines by a system of working groups, who are given tasks which they share out among themselves. The Swedish motor firm Volvo have found that it pays them to do this because of the greater interest taken in the job and the more responsible attitudes to it. We are learning by experience that it does not pay to treat men as machines rather than as human beings.

(*c*) *The problem of incentives and efficiency*

All of this brings us back to the relationship, touched on several times already, between incentives and efficiency.

The market system seeks to ensure efficiency by enlisting the strong forces of self-interest. Customers spend their income on different goods in order to maximize their satisfaction. Workers sell their labour and skills to employers in order to get the best wages, business firms fix output and prices, and combine labour, capital and materials, in such a way as to maximize profits.

Up to a point, this is very successful. If there is an excess of railway porters and a shortage of coal miners, then the earnings of porters should fall and those of the miners rise and this should attract labour from one job to the other and so use it more efficiently. The same applies as between teachers and doctors, or whatever. We have already seen in chapter 4 how many obstacles there are to this adjustment working smoothly.

In general, however, if goods are being produced and sold at a reasonable, but not excessive, profit, this is prima facie evidence that resources are being used efficiently in making what people want. More strongly, if goods are made and sold at a loss, there is reason to believe that resources are being wastefully used relative to what people want.

But the regulating function of competition and the price system work far from perfectly. It is all too easy for firms to be in a position to make profits because they control markets, and there are no competitors who are able to force them to be efficient, or because it pays a group of firms to collude tacitly in keeping up prices and competing by means of advertising and product differentiation. Moreover, it is in terms of private costs and private benefits that profits are made and losses avoided, not social costs and benefits. Thus the private car owner takes his car into the city centre because the money cost he has to pay in petrol, maintenance and tax does not fully reflect the cost of the congestion which he causes to others, while the local bus or railway service makes a loss because the fares it charges cannot reflect the social benefits of reduced congestion without going so high as to choke off passenger demand.

On the other hand, the command principle, if it operates in the strict sense of ordering enterprises to produce a prescribed list of goods, using prescribed quantities and qualities of resources, goes to the other extreme. It provides no incentive other than a patriotic desire to fulfil the plan or a fear of the consequences of not doing so. It provides no criteria by which to judge whether resources are in fact being used efficiently, other than that of compliance with the planners' estimate of what is appropriate, and these are only too liable to be upset by unforeseen events. And, as we have stressed, if prices are not allowed to change with demand and supply variations, there is no feedback from consumers to producers.

Most people would probably accept that it is usually best to pay people money incomes and leave them free to buy goods and services for themselves in the shops, according to how they want to divide their money between them. In general, people are better judges of their own wants than any public body can be. Provided incomes are not too unequal, any attempt at allocation or rationing can only be justified in times of acute shortages of necessities, such as wartime. But we have to accept that there are certain services, like education and medical treatment, which are better provided free and paid for out of taxation, even though it is perfectly possible to sell them for a price in the market. In these cases the social benefit of everyone having access to a similar standard of service without barrier of means is held to outweigh any possible social cost in interfering with individual preferences.

In the organization of industry and business there is a strong case for making use of the criterion of profitability. If a firm is making a profit, or at any rate avoiding a loss, this is a clear and definite indicator of success to its management, and the pursuit of profit gives them a well-defined target to aim for. The problem is to find some wider framework, within which profit seeking can be carried out, which will as far as possible ensure that overall social interests are being followed. Attempts have been made to do this by policies directed against monopolies and restrictive practices. In Britain, for instance, the government has powers to have firms which dominate an industry, or mergers which may create a dominant position, investigated through the Monopolies Commission. There is not much evidence of success in stopping the trend towards larger firms, if only because the economies of scale so often work towards a larger size. Most restrictive practices, such as price fixing and market sharing agreements, have been banned. In the United States there is a more ambitious policy of regarding certain monopolistic practices as illegal and prosecuting firms under the Anti-Trust Acts, but again only with limited effect.

If firms are determined not to compete in ways which give the consumer a cheaper and better product, it is not easy to make them do so. In practice, the most effective competition tends to come from firms in other industries, who break into a sheltered market by means of technical innovation, producing a new and improved product more cheaply and thus undercutting established positions. Now the trend in Britain is rather to accept the large firm as inevitable and indeed essential, because of the economies of scale, and for the government to seek to enter into partnership with them, as with the proposed National Enterprise Board and planning agreements.

But how far does the criterion of profitability imply the incentive of profit? How far, in particular, does it imply the incentive of individual gain? Already in modern business the tycoon in pursuit of personal fortune is the exception. The typical member of top management tends to see the success of the firm, whether measured by profits, or sales, or technical leadership, as something independent of his personal income. He is rarely a large shareholder in it. Salary is as much a badge of status as a means of spending more money, and many other motives come in, such as professional esteem, interest in building up a business, ideals of public service and the like. The same is even more true of those whose work is in the public services or the professions.

How far can we look to see a situation where men and women work, not to get more money, but out of some such ideal as public service? Christians cannot but have this as an ideal. They must constantly point out that it is unlikely that a system based primarily on self-seeking will lead to harmony and justice, and that the health of society demands that self be transcended by a higher loyalty. Yet it would be unreasonable to build too many hopes on this being practicable as a general rule. Many jobs are dull and uninteresting and only the most dedicated could find much satisfaction in them other than the pay. Most people, though they can be moved to idealism if their imagination is caught, are bound up in their own affairs and in the struggle to pay their bills and give their families a reasonable standard of living.

Even if all were convinced and committed Christians, which is unlikely enough, it is not certain that the pursuit of money and what it can buy would cease to have any influence, for men can so easily deceive themselves about their motives. And even if money is not the first aim, other things like power and influence are equally strong incentives, and ones to which committed men are more prone. It is well known how dedicated men and women, in the church or voluntary agencies, can seek power and authority and struggle to get their own way, in the sincere belief that by doing so they are enabling themselves to promote the cause more effectively.

There is also the point that if we do not use pay differentials to attract men to and from jobs, some other method must be found. Given men's mixed motives, it is probably best that they should be induced to seek the jobs in which they can do their most fruitful work by the inducement of higher pay, and be steered away from those where their services are less needed, by lower earnings rates. The only feasible alternative would be some sort of direction by higher authority, as was used in wartime, and this is bound to be arbitrary and wasteful. The provisos must be that the degree of inequality of rewards between different jobs is not too great, that there do not exist too high barriers to keep those with suitable talents from getting access to the jobs where these can be used, and that relative rates of pay for different jobs bear some relation to relative degrees of skill, responsibility and net advantages.

(*d*) *How to combine enterprise and initiative with social control*

In terms of industrial and commercial organization the key issue is how to combine enterprise and initiative with social control. Business managements must have the kind of freedom which private enterprise has in the past ensured, of being able to spot new types of demand which can be met, new products which can be developed, new processes which can be devised to make products more cheaply. They must be free to take up such opportunities without having to go through endless bureaucratic channels to get approval. They must be prepared to take risks and be able to get hold of the capital which will enable them to do so. If the risk comes off, the public benefits, but if it fails, someone has to stand the loss.

Yet this freedom of enterprise and initiative must be within the framework of social control. There must be some means of ensuring that it does not involve unacceptable social costs, through pollution, or through throwing large numbers of workers out of a job with no provision of alternative employment, or through enabling excessive profits to be made out of all proportion to the benefits conferred on the public. If competition in a market economy cannot be relied upon to ensure this, some alternative must be found.

The experience of the nationalized industries illustrates the difficulty of striking this balance. The principle on which they were set up was that the Boards would be free to act as commercial enterprises, within the guidelines of general policy which the government would lay down to protect the public interest in such essential industries as transport and fuel and power. In fact successive governments long failed to give the Boards clear guidelines on general policy, while constantly interfering in detailed decisions, for short-term political reasons. Thus they have often vetoed price increases necessary to cover rising costs, or have cut the nationalized industries' investment plans whenever they have felt it necessary to restrict public spending. At the same time, vast investment projects were often approved with very little appraisal of their prospective returns as against alternative uses of capital.

Fairly definite guidelines were laid down in the White Papers of 1961 and 1967.[6] Prices of nationalized services were to be based as far as possible on marginal costs, that is on the additional costs incurred in providing each service. New investment was to be appraised against a target rate of return comparable to that achieved on capital in the private sector. Overall, the undertakings were given target annual rates of earnings on their capital at which to aim as an incentive to efficiency. Even these criteria, the details of which have been criticized,[7] have been overcome by events. During the rapid inflation of 1972–74, the government tried to strengthen its price control measures by refusing to allow price increases in the public sector in line with costs, and providing large subsidies to meet the deficits.

Thus even within the public sector it has been difficult to combine commercial freedom with social control. In the private sector, where the aims of firms to maximize their profits or their sales can conflict directly with government aims, there has been less experience to go on. In pursuit of their overall policies of holding the balance of the economy, governments have, it is true, devised certain methods of acting directly on individual firms, as well as on the general level of demand in the economy. Thus they seek to encourage or discourage investment by firms by altering the terms on which they are given corporation tax deductions on their capital spending, or sometimes cash grants. They also use tax allowances and cash grants and other methods to encourage firms to invest in the development and similar areas where they want to encourage new industry.

In some countries there has been a tradition of close co-operation between government and industry in working out economic policy. This has been especially important in Japan, where business firms are very responsive to suggestions by the government as to whether investment should be expanded or contracted, or what kinds of exports should be developed. In France there is a similar tradition of close co-operation and active government intervention, and government financial institutions are also a large source of investment capital. These factors made possible the system of indicative planning, by which target rates of output for each industry and for the economy as a whole were worked out in collaboration by the government planners and industrial organizations. The only serious attempt at this in Britain, the National Plan of

1965, suffered from being worked out far too hastily and was never really accepted by industry. In any case its target of a sustained annual rate of growth of a little under 4% had to be abandoned in 1966, when the immediate need to protect the balance of payments led to severe deflationary measures which slowed down growth.

It remains to be seen whether the present government's plans for a closer partnership, based on a government provision of capital to industrial firms in return for a share in the equity, and planning agreements by which large companies co-ordinate their development plans with government long-term policies, will be more successful. In their favour is the recognized need for a greater role for the government if the problems of overcoming inflation and improving industrial efficiency are to be overcome. Working against them is a fear that governments tend to be too much dominated by short-term political considerations and hence find it difficult to pursue consistent long-term policies. There is also a suspicion among business leaders that the government, despite its protestations, is hostile to private enterprise and too much under the influence of the trade unions.

(*e*) *The future of the joint stock company*

Bound up with all this is the future of the joint stock company, or business corporation, the characteristic business unit of the modern market economy. The ordinary shareholders are the nominal owners of the company and have the right to vote at annual general meetings. Most of them inevitably know little and care less about how it is run, so long as their dividends are satisfactory and their shares keep up their capital value. Provided they can keep their shareholders happy and avert takeovers, the directors are effectively responsible to no one. In particular, they have no legal obligation to consider the interests of any other parties, such as the firm's employees, or its customers, or the general public, except in so far as they are bound by specific legal enactments, such as the need to observe safety regulations, or to make redundancy payments, or to avoid unjustified dismissals. There have been cases where a Board has wanted to give more generous compensation to employees on the winding up of a company than the law required, and have been prevented from doing so by shareholders, who had the only legal claim on the assets.[8]

It has often been argued that the legal status of companies should be altered to give them wider responsibilities, though how these could be made effective in the case of the customers or the general public is hard to see. So far as employees are concerned, there are moves in many countries to give them a voice in the running of the company. They take two forms, the setting up of works councils and similar bodies at different levels from the department or shop upwards, and the appointment of worker's representatives to the boards.

Consultative councils of various sorts have been common. In some countries, as in West Germany, these are obligatory, while in Britain they are provided for by statute in the nationalized industries. It is difficult, however, to make them very effective. They tend to become concerned largely with trivialities such as the oft-quoted canteen tea, or with personal grievances over working conditions. Any attempt at a more constructive use comes up against the obstacles of apathy by the rank and file of workers, fears of trade unionists of the usurping of the rights of collective bargaining machinery, and unwillingness by the management to give up their prerogatives of responsibility for business decisions, which may often involve confidential issues of trade prospects not for the ears of their competitors. There is also the problem of how they should be elected, whether by all the workers in each establishment covered, or through the trade unions. The latter naturally prefer this, since they regard themselves as the natural voice of the workers, but in many cases the local union hierarchy may not effectively represent the views of the rank and file.

The appointment of workers' representatives to the boards has gone furthest in West Germany, where it is obligatory to have them on the supervisory board, which is the upper of the two boards which German companies have, and is concerned with questions of general policy rather than day-to-day business management. In France the boards of the nationalized industries have to have workers' representatives to the extent of one-third. At this level it is normal for these to be chosen by the trade unions.

The main problem is what status these representatives should have. Should they act mainly as watchdogs for the employees' interests, or should they take a full part in forming company policy along with the other directors? If they do this, will they then cease to be regarded by the employees as representing their interests and be thought of as just another of the bosses, much as the ex-trade union officials are who serve in a personal capacity on the boards of the British nationalized industries?

More important, because more subtle, than these formal provisions, is the attitude of all those who work for a company at all levels, towards the company which claims such a large share of their lives. There is, of course, an inherent conflict of interest between the bulk of the employees, whether blue collar or white collar, and the top management. The former are bound to be concerned primarily with their own personal situation, with their pay, their promotion prospects and working conditions, the interest or otherwise of the job, personal relationships in their own department. They are apt to look at the bosses in terms of how much they can get out of them in return for how much in the way of work. The top management, on the other hand, see the firm as the embodiment of their own careers and become committed to its commercial and technical success. They are inevitably led to think of the workforce in terms of the amount of output to be got for a given level of labour costs and to see enlightened labour relations primarily as a means towards better financial results.

One is bound to ask whether it is out of the question to imagine a business firm eliciting the kind of loyalty and sharing of ideals from all its employees that, say, a non-profit-making organization like a school, or a hospital, or a charity, or a church can hope to do. In these cases there are sometimes disputes over pay and conditions, but they are mitigated by a shared concern for common objectives. Can a business company, dedicated primarily to supplying goods and services to be sold to the public on the most profitable terms, and working in competition with other companies in a struggle for markets, possibly elicit the same kind of loyalty? Is it desirable that it should?

There are obvious dangers here. Some of the best intentioned managements in the past, who have gone out of their way to give their workers good conditions, including sports and social clubs, housing, medical services and the like, have also engendered an atmosphere of paternalism that many of their employees find oppressive. Nor would one want to hold a brief for the 'organization man', more common in American experience, who is expected to devote his whole life, and often those of his wife and family also, heart and soul to the greater success of the corporation which employs him.

There are dangers of another sort also. A too easy acceptance of the belief that 'we are all working together for the common good', especially if it involves tacit collusion with competitors, can result in a kind of easy-going inefficiency which results in good wages for the staff and good dividends for the shareholders at the expense of high prices and poor service to the consumers. Yet if firms are to give efficient service to the public, they may have to be ruthless in cutting out featherbedding and inefficiency among their employees, and will not be able to guarantee them the security of doing the same job in the way they have always done it.

It is difficult to elicit whole-hearted loyalty and a sense of belonging and working together for an undertaking which is primarily concerned with profit for the shareholders or high salaries for the bosses. But nationalization, replacing the private shareholders with the general public as nominal owners, and embodying an explicit obligation to consider the public interest, has not so far shown that it can make much difference to this in practice.

6. *What light can be thrown on the problem from Christian understanding?*

The kind of dilemmas we have been discussing cannot be neatly resolved. There must remain an inevitable tension between the need to give incentives to individuals to give of their best and the need to secure the wider interests of the community, the need to give scope to business enterprise and initiative and the need to ensure that overall priorities are followed.

The Christian understanding can help towards effective action in this field, since it reminds us that such tension is of the essence of human life. In a limited and imperfect world, if we push any argument to what looks like its logical conclusion, we are likely to get into an extreme position which does violence to alternative aspects of a truth which is too great and varied to be encompassed in our formulas. This should breed a certain humility and willingness to recognize that one may be mistaken, or biased by one's personal interests or prejudices.

Christian thinking can also make more positive contributions towards making these tensions fruitful in mutual understanding and enrichment, rather than merely destructive. They include the following:

(*a*) *Recognition of the value of all persons*

The Christian faith reminds us constantly that all persons, whatever their positions or views, are of infinite value. Hencc they must not be treated merely as instruments or units, and any form of organization which so treats them comes under condemnation. Moreover, each person has his or her unique contribution to make to the common welfare, and any system which stultifies this is impoverishing the life of the whole community. This is often very difficult to live up to in practice, in the large-scale complex economic and political organizations of modern society. It must remain the norm, however, by which all business firms, or workplaces, or political parties, or government departments, or schools or hospitals or whatever must be judged.

(*b*) *Combining responsibility and authority with humility and consideration*

Another important contribution which Christians should be making is that of showing that the necessary exercise of responsibility and authority can be combined with humility and consideration. In varying degrees in all walks of life there must be leaders who have the responsibility for taking decisions about how their part of the system will work and who must exercise authority over those who are placed under them. These positions must not be shirked, and where clear judgments and decisive rulings are called for, they must be given. But it is possible to do this with the humility which recognizes that this responsibility is a trust, not a privilege, that those who exercise it are still unworthy, though they are doing their best, that they do it as servants of the community rather than lords seeking deference. It is possible also to do it with consideration, for those placed under one, their difficulties and problems as well as their strengths, for those whom the organization serves, for the wider community.

Many non-Christians put many Christians to shame in the way in which they do this, but Christians who serve the one who came as a servant though he was Lord of all have a stronger motivation to recognize and apply it. As part of this combination of responsibility and humility should also go a recognition of one's own fallibility. The best and most conscientious of us are unlikely to exercise absolute power without abuse. Hence there is always a need for checks and balances. Our decisions must be subjected to approval or disapproval. This may come formally, from superior office-holders or committees within an organization, or from the political structure. Or it may come informally, from the general public when they refuse to buy our firm's products and it goes bankrupt.

Those who find themselves in positions of responsibility tend to chafe at these restrictions, and feel that any questioning of their plans is pettifogging, or has ulterior motives. Christians should be able to be more critical of their own motives and more ready to admit that they can be mistaken.

(*c*) *The proper role of wealth and power*

Inherent in all this discussion is the proper use of wealth and power. As we saw in the last chapter, there is a legitimate pursuit of wealth, in the sense of good stewardship, of making more responsible and efficient use of resources to increase the means available for meeting men's needs. In a world which is still basically poor, this aim has to be pursued, and our study of the economic order is concerned to see how it can be done most effectively. It is in this connection that we consider the part which the search for higher pay, or for business profits, can play as incentives and criteria.

Similarly, with the use of power. The purpose of political power, at all levels from leadership of a business firm, a club, a charity or a church, up to that of members of Parliament and cabinet ministers, is to get things done by collective action in order to promote the greater benefit of the people. Just as desire for money can be an incentive towards an efficient use of material resources, so ambition for power and prestige can be an incentive to get into a position where one can take effective action.

But there is only too much evidence of how both these drives can be abused, and neither the working of the market economy nor the checks and balances of democratic politics are by themselves adequate means of preventing abuse. The Christian insight has a contribution to make here by insisting that the pursuit of wealth and of power cannot be safely treated as ends in themselves, but only as means towards the more effective loving of the neighbour, through the structures of the economic and political order.

But if Christians are to say this, they must take it seriously. They must hold their own motives and actions under judgment. They must be ready to question the reasons which lead them either to seek or to avoid positions of greater income and greater power. Am I seeking this post because I genuinely feel it is the one in which I can do the best service, the one to which I am called? Or, on the other hand, am I avoiding a position of wealth or power in which I could do good work just because I fear to be thought self-seeking and worldly, or using the cloak of unworldliness as a cover for shrinking from a position of whose responsibilities I am afraid? There can be mixed motives in holding back as well as in thrusting forward.

Above all, as Christians we must take the use of wealth and power seriously. Too often, we are inclined to regard them as dirty and contaminating and shrink back into a comfortable private world of limited aims and limited usefulness, in which we can avoid the moral tensions which active involvement in the world must bring. Yet the proper acquisition and use of material wealth and power are inescapable issues in any society. They would arise just as much, and pose just as many problems, in an alternative 'Christian' society, were that possible, as they do in the very mixed world in which we live. Many experimental idealistic communities have broken down on this stubborn fact.

(*d*) *What kind of society?*

In the light of all these problems, what kind of society should we be looking for? We shall be going into this question more fully in the next chapter, but certain observations may be helpful.

There is undoubtedly a need for experiments in alternative and more idealistic methods of organizing the production and distribution of goods and services. We need to see more communes and other self-supporting groups based on agriculture and small-scale industry. We also need to see more producers' co-operatives, in which the organization of production is carried out on a partnership basis by all those engaged in the enterprise.

Not that there have not been plenty of these in the past,[9] and most of them have come adrift on the obstinate facts of conflicts of ideals as to how they should be run, or clashes of personality between those taking a leading role in them. There is a real need, therefore, to regard them as a kind of laboratory experiment, in which the different ways of tackling the issues of incentives and criteria for efficiency, or the right use of wealth and power, can be studied.

But experience suggests that these alternative forms of organization are likely to be small scale; indeed, the success of most of them has depended on their remaining small. The effective and responsible working of the mainstream of the community's economic organizations is always likely to be more important. For us in the West, this means starting with the mixed economy as we know it, getting clearer about the nature of its problems, trying to see how they can be overcome. This involves two lines of approach. First, a fuller study of the possibilities of closer co-operation between the government and business firms, to see how far the system can evolve in the direction of combining flexibility and enterprise with fuller participation and greater social responsibility. Secondly, it means looking at possible alternative systems, such as the various forms of socialist economies, and appraising equally seriously their potential efficiency in tackling the same problems.

There is enough here for all of us, in terms of his own experience and opportunities, whether we are business men, or shop floor or office workers, or professionals, or politicians, or academics, or simply concerned members of the general public.

8

Conclusions on a Christian Approach to the Economic Order

1. *Contrasts of success and failure*

Our case studies of different aspects of the world economy have revealed marked contrasts of light and shade, good and evil, success and failure.

The post-war world saw nearly thirty years of success in achieving a rapid rate of economic growth, a remarkable rise in the living standards of ordinary people in the industrial countries, the maintenance of full employment and a rapid expansion of world trade. Most of the restrictions which had clogged the channels of trade in the thirties were removed. On the other hand, the underlying tensions were not resolved, and they led to a steady building up of inflation to a point where it threatened stable growth, a slump in world trade with rising unemployment, and growing instability both in industrial relations and in the political system.

We have also seen the general acceptance of the ideal of the Welfare State, a massive extension of the social services and public responsibility for ensuring that all have a reasonable income and reasonable opportunities. On the other hand we find that expenditure on these services is outrunning the willingness of the public to pay for them in taxation, that considerable poverty and inequality remain and that there is sharp controversy on what the role of the social services should be.

Turning to the wider world, we have seen a revolution of rising aspirations among the peoples of the developing countries, considerable success by many of them in keeping their incomes rising faster than their populations, and an acceptance by the rich countries in principle of the responsibility for helping them through aid and trade. On the other hand we find the poverty of the masses in the Third World hardly dented, and that progress towards effectively breaking out of it is impeded both by political factors within the developing countries, and by unwillingness by the rich countries to give up their superior power in world trade.

The chapter on growth revealed contrasts even more marked. We have seen that economic growth responsibly considered is a part of good stewardship and represents a potential for the more effective and constructive meeting of human wants. We have seen that the obstacles to the feasibility of continued growth, arising from the danger of population outstripping food supply, from the exhaustion of non-reproducible resources, and from pollution of the environment, though they present serious problems, are not incapable of being overcome. Yet growth pursued as an end in itself can lead to greed, exploitation, injustice and a squandering of the world's resources.

Finally, we have seen that these contradictions and tensions go right through the economic order, whether it is organized mainly on the market principle or on the command principle. On the one hand there is the need to encourage enterprise and initiative, to give incentives to use resources efficiently and to provide criteria by which to judge whether they are being so used. On the other hand there is the need to provide some means of protecting the community from exploitation, of ensuring that wider social interests are taken into account, and also of making it possible for men and women to participate meaningfully in the work by which they get their living.

Christians will not be surprised at this record of contrasts. It is what we would expect from what we know of human nature. Men have the potentiality of great achievement once their imagination is aroused and their loyalties inspired, but equally of great greed, injustice and neglect of the interests of others, once their self-seeking nature is allowed to pull them down. We believe that in Christ we have the word of hope which points the way out of these contradictions, but it is up to us to work out what this should mean in terms of the way in which the economic order is organized.

2. *The revolution of rising expectations*

None of this is new, of course; indeed, it is the age-old human story. But it is given a new force and immediacy by the revolution of rising expectations. Those who are poor and ignorant and under-privileged are no longer prepared to accept their subordinate position as ordained of God and part of the nature of things. This is true both of the less privileged within the rich countries and of the less privileged majority of the world's people in the developing countries. The continuance of great inequalities of wealth and of power are no longer accepted in a world where it is believed that technical progress now gives us the capability of producing enough to enable all to have a better life, provided we can use natural resources and human skills responsibly. Unlike the position in the past, it is now reasonable to expect that poverty and injustice ought to be able to be overcome.

At the same time the better off and more privileged feel themselves to be threatened. The comfortable, cultured middle-class way of life based on plenty of cheap labour has now gone. Cherished differentials in pay are being eroded, council estates are engulfing the middle-class suburbs, crowds of vulgar tourists throng formerly select holiday resorts, subsidized fee-paying schools give way to comprehensives, and so on. Out of this kind of clash come many of the very real conflicts of our day, from strikes and political protests to urban guerillas and the tensions between the West and the Third World.

3. *The need to rise to the challenge of the times*

(*a*) *An exciting new world*

The world we live in nowadays is in many ways uncertain, perplexing and even frightening, but it is also exciting, challenging and full of potentialities. Old structures are breaking up, old ways of thought cracking, and new ideas and new experiments are all around us. As has often been said, man has come of age, and men must use the vast powers which modern knowledge and technology give us to shape a destiny for themselves.

Christians, who believe that this is God's world, in which he is active and of which he is in charge, should welcome this and be ready to respond positively to it. We believe that God is working a work in the world, for those with eyes to see. He is always doing so, of course, but perhaps in more striking and unexpected ways today. It is up to us to see what he is doing and hear what he is saying to us about what he would have us do, in the furthering of his purposes.

(*b*) *The need for understanding, responsibility and commitment*

If we are to do this, we need understanding and commitment. The temptation comes to all of us to take fright at the vastness of the movements around us, and to try to retreat into a comfortable private world of home and job, family, friends and recreations, and familiar Sunday worship.

But it is being made increasingly clear to us that there can be no security in any of these things, however sacred and precious. In small ways we are finding this already even in countries like our own, when inflation threatens our standard of living and strikes disrupt our public services, and there is little we can do to counter them. And we are all too well aware that many are less secure than we are, as near as Belfast or Londonderry, not to mention Saigon or Jerusalem or Beirut or Salisbury, Rhodesia, or Lisbon. If we have eyes to see and ears to hear, surely God is bringing home to us Christ's teaching that he who would save his life shall lose it and he who loses it shall find it (Matt. 16.25; Luke 17.33; John 12.25). Not that we must wantonly give up home, job, family and friends, for these are given to us to serve, cherish and enjoy. Rather it is that we cannot find our security in them, still less in the placid, unshaken, orderly rhythm of suburban life, nor in the unquestioned simplicities of conventional churchmanship. Only in God and his service can we find a security strong enough to withstand the shaking of the foundations.[1]

So we are called first to understand what is going on in the world. The purpose of our analysis of practical problems in chapters 3 to 7 has been to make some contribution towards helping people to do this. We need to know why inflation has become such a menace, what causes it, how the hopes and fears and aspirations and the policies of governments are bound up in it. We need to know why we still have poverty in the midst of affluence and what can effectively be done to overcome it. And similarly with the contrast between rich and poor in the wider world, the problem of economic growth and its limitations, and the frictions and tensions which are inherent in the working of any sort of economic system. Only on a basis of sound knowledge of the facts can we make our choices in an enlightened and not merely in a prejudiced way.

Understanding is also necessary at a deeper level. We need to know not merely the facts of the situation, but also their inner meaning, in terms of men's hopes and fears and aspirations, in terms of what we believe to be the truth about the nature of the universe and of men and women in it. As Christians we have a great need to make our faith come alive in these terms. So often there is a big gap between the theology which we profess in church and try to live by in our personal conduct, and our actions and beliefs in the economic and political fields. We believe that this is God's world, that he has made us for himself and redeemed us in Christ, that he calls for a response from us of love and trust which has to be worked out in terms of right living at all levels of life. We have to try to work out what this means in the way in which we do our work, or run our business, or protect our interests in our trade union, in the way we vote, the party we support and our beliefs about what government policy should be. It is only as we do this that our faith can become real to ourselves and, through our witness, real to those all around us who desperately need an understanding of life by which to live.

So understanding must be accompanied by responsibility. Whether we like it or not, we are all neighbours and we are our brothers' keepers. My neighbour is my Marxist colleague whose views I detest, or my friend who seems to have no interest except in making money, or my other friends and acquaintances who are bound up in improving their homes, or drinking at the club. My neighbour is the shop steward in Coventry who is always causing strikes, or the poor peasant in India or Brazil, or the nationalist politician in Kenya, or the Arab terrorist in Lebanon or the Soviet bureaucrat in Moscow. Hard though it may be to understand them and all the others (and hard though they may find it to understand us), we have a responsibility to them which we cannot back out of. The purely private, comfortable life is not for the Christian.

Thus responsibilty involves commitment. If we call ourselves Christians, we are committed to seeing that God's will is done in the world, to the best of our ability. As we saw in chapter 2 and as we shall see in more detail in the next section, there are wide differences among Christians as to what this should mean in practice. But it must at least mean that we start from a vision of a world of which the essential nature is love and goodness and justice, and in which love and goodness and justice have won the decisive victory over hatred and evil and oppression. But the victory which they have won is that of self-giving sacrifice, not of self-assertion, and so the way of commitment must always be in the spirit of Christ.

Is this too much for us? Many readers may feel appalled at this point. 'What can I do? I am only a simple fellow, not an economist or a political scientist. I have a hard enough struggle getting a living and looking after my family. I can't be expected to understand all about inflation, poverty, the Third World, growth, the future of the mixed economy and the like.'

Three things must be said. First, our commitment is to serve where we are and as we are. We are to use our gifts, experience and opportunities to the full and to try to act responsibly and lovingly in the situation which faces us. We are not called to use knowledge, gifts or opportunities which we have not got, but neither are we to make our limitations the excuse for not doing our best where we are.

Secondly, the motivation for our commitment is love. We are not called to serve the world in obedience to the arbitrary commands of a potentate sitting up above the skies, who will punish us if we are negligent. Our loving our neighbours and service of them to the best of our abilities is the response of love to the God whom we know as loving Father. Once we have come to know something of the wonder and the depth of the love of God as we see it in Christ, we cannot be satisfied with less than this response. Once we have seen this vision and known this truth, a life of self-seeking evasion of the challenge seems flat and unsatisfying and stultifying.

Thirdly, we are not called upon to do all this in our own strength or wisdom. The Christian knows a God who manifests himself as three persons, not only above us and with us, but in us. The Christian life is a sharing of the life of God through the Holy Spirit and we can trust in his power and his guidance. This we can know individually through our prayer and devotion, but still more corporately as we seek to join with others in understanding his purposes and doing his will. It is not that he supersedes our natural understanding with flashes of miraculous information from outside, rather that new insights and understandings come to us as we think about the world's problems in the light of his truth. Nor does his strength come to us from outside before we decide to do what we feel God is calling us to do; rather we experience it as we go forward in faith in spite of the consciousness of our weakness. But very real it has been proved to be.

4. *The varying responses*

The actual form that commitment to responsible love will take will vary greatly, between Christians as between holders of other types of world view. Differences in temperament and experience, in theological tradition and in position in life all affect our understanding of this. Among the innumerable shades of opinion, however, it is useful to distinguish three characteristic dominant modes of response; those of withdrawal, of revolution and of involvement.

(*a*) *Withdrawal*

Some people, looking at the world with its disorders, injustices, greed and oppression, and comparing it with the ideal of the kingdom of God, are led to conclude that the Christian response must be one of withdrawal. They feel that the world's economic and political structures are so corrupted by self-seeking and so resistent to the love of God, that the only thing to do is to break free of them and try to create alternative structures which will embody the kingdom more faithfully.

This attitude must be distinguished from the kind of head-in-sand withdrawal from responsibility into a private world which we have just been criticizing. The type of withdrawal we are now considering is in principle not one of escape but one of positive commitment. It will find expression typically in small-scale alternative communities, where Christians try to live together, growing their own food as far as possible, perhaps engaging in craft work or small-scale industry, sometimes aiming at self-sufficiency, in other cases rather at trading with the outside world. They try to work out within the life of a group of neighbours and friends the answers to the sort of questions we were discussing in chapter 7, as well as the personal, social and political problems of living and working together.

There is no doubt that there is a very real place for such experimental communities. We need the experience which those who take part in them can give to the rest of us, as well as the living examples of how problems can be tackled and relationships established.

Yet it is fairly clear that for most of us this cannot be the way. Of course, it is impracticable, for most of us cannot opt out of jobs, homes, neighbourhoods and civic duties in this way. But is it really the answer? If God's will is to be done in the world, it must be done in and through the economic structure by which we get our living, and the political structure by which our relationships are regulated. Most of the world must go to work in factory, office or farm, live in town or village, be citizens of Britain, the United States, India or Nigeria or whatever. They cannot opt out, and should we seek to do so?

(*b*) *Revolution*

A second attitude, which is perhaps more common outside the church than within it, but which has its Christian antecedents, is that of revolution. This also looks at the contrast between the actual society and the ideal and sees the actual as being so corrupt as to have little hope of reform. The response, however, is not to withdraw and build alternative societies, but rather to work from within for the overthrowing of the corrupt system, so that it can be replaced by something better.

Naturally, those who take this view tend to be mostly of the Left and deeply influenced by Marxism in one form or another, though there is also a nationalist, populist right-wing revolutionary tradition, which has survived the discrediting of Fascism. Whatever their ideology, revolutionaries tend to see the breakdown of the existing system as inevitable, and hence regard it as the lesser of two evils to work to further this breakdown. Some would hope to achieve this by peaceful means, but many would regard this as impossible and be prepared to use violence.

Few Christians in Britain are attracted to the revolutionary approach, for generations of Liberal democracy are in our blood. Yet there is a challenge to us here, to take seriously the evils and injustices in our society which we are all too apt to condone, and to see that they may be so serious that they could lead to breakdown. Nor is it surprising that in many parts of the world, notably in Latin America or among non-whites in South Africa, Christians faced with entrenched injustices in the fabric of society have been led to feel that revolution is the only answer.

Christians of all beliefs must therefore be ready to enter into dialogue with those who hold a revolutionary position, to be open to their insights and to try to discuss seriously with them the moral choices such a position involves. For there is undoubtedly a debit side, which it is our duty to point out. Once we accept breakdown as inevitable, we become committed to working to accelerate it. This means a sharpening of conflicts rather than a search for peace, a setting up of revolutionaries in confrontation with the authorities, rather than the seeking of understanding and accommodation with them. It tends to lead on to the using of conspiratorial methods, an acceptance that the end justifies the means, a willingness to distort and pervert evidence to strengthen a partisan case. It can lead to intolerance of opponents and a desire to suppress their views by force, and the kind of mindless chanting of slogans that is so often a substitute for thought among popular revolutionary movements.

If the use of violence comes to be accepted as inevitable and justified, the dangers are of course still greater. We have plenty of examples today of the ugly results of sincere and passionate belief allied to the use of violence, whether in Northern Ireland, or among the Palestine Liberation Movement, or the urban guerillas of South America, or left-wing idealists in Germany. Any violence can breed equal violence in defence among the authorities, and the ultimate casualty can be political freedom itself. Moreover, as we mentioned earlier, those who take power through violent revolution tend to find themselves locked into a situation where they have to use violent repression to maintain themselves in power.[2]

(*c*) *Involvement*

The instinct of probably most Christians in Britain and the West that the Liberal political tradition is not yet dead is still a sound one. It leads to a third attitude, of involvement or participation. This begins by accepting that the economic and political structures of our society, with all their faults and limitations and injustices, are not so corrupt that we must write them off. There is enough of good in the mixed economy and in parliamentary democracy to make it worth our while accepting them as means through which God's will can be carried out. It is possible to work within the structures, along with all men and women of goodwill, to modify them and make them more appropriate instruments through which justice can be done and the love of the neighbour expressed.

This has been the dominant theme of this book and is probably the position which most of its readers will find congenial. Certain warnings must, however, be given.

First, this approach calls for active involvement, not for being content to sit and criticize on the sidelines. In accordance with the opportunities which each of us has, we must be prepared to take up positions, advocate policies and work for them. We have got to get in and be prepared to get our hands dirty.

Secondly, any effective action will involve compromise. We shall not be able to attain the ideal result which we should like, whether it is in reorganizing the structure of companies to make them more responsible, or in overcoming poverty among the old, or in getting a more effective partnership for world development between rich and poor countries, or in improving the environment. We are always up against the obstinate facts of the situation, such as limited resources in money or manpower, or the strongly held views of people we have to work with, whom we cannot force to our way of thinking. The aim must be to achieve the best possible, rather than the ideal. Compromise in this sense is not a suspect flirting with evil, but a worthy aim.

Thirdly, the holders of the two earlier views serve to remind us that there may come points at which compromise ceases to be of this sort. There may be questions of principle on which we must stand firm and say so, for instance when those we are trying to work with want us to do something that is so unjust, or arbitrary, or dishonest, that it will destroy any good which it may be designed to achieve. Not all will judge where this point comes in the same way, and we must be charitable both to those who take a more rigorous view than we do, and to those who seem more lax. But come it probably will for all.

5. *The policy implications of the third choice*

If we accept this third type of response, what are likely to be its implications in terms of policy? What kinds of social and economic developments ought we to be working towards? The following may be suggested as arising out of the kind of investigation of practical problems which we have conducted.

(*a*) *A closer partnership between private enterprise and the government*

This would seem to be essential if we are to retain the initiative and flexibility of private enterprise while overcoming its irresponsibility, limited horizons and inequality. At the same time we want to extend the planning role of the government without giving way to the rigidity and arbitrariness of a planned economy.

But if progress is to be made in this direction, it can only be through a real partnership, and that means a willingness of each side to accept and understand the other. Governments must accept that business firms need a clear field of commercial freedom to engage in profitable enterprise, while rightly insisting that they should exercise this within an agreed framework of overall economic policy. Business firms must accept that the government has a legitimate and inescapable concern for the welfare of the whole community, and therefore has the right to ensure that business operates for the benefit of all groups, employees, customers, the general public, and not merely shareholders or top management.

What this will mean in practice has yet to be worked out, but goodwill is essential. Christians who are active in business, politics or the trade unions have an important role to play here in working for this goodwill and helping to bring about mutual understanding. A particular contribution which they should be able to offer is the ability to criticize their own motives and prejudices and to enter imaginatively into the motives and prejudices of others.

(*b*) *An effort towards greater public understanding of economic issues*

If such a partnership is to be possible, there is also a need for a greater understanding of economic issues at all levels of public life. For reasons which we discussed in chapter 1, Christians have not made as great a contribution to this as they should be able to do, through their understanding of human nature and human society. One would hope to see them taking the same kind of lead in the discussion of economic issues like inflation, the balance of payments, industrial relations, international trade or the organization of industry, as they have done over social issues such as abortion, divorce, gambling and drink, or educational policy.

Such a process of public discussion is unlikely to arrive at agreement, for differences of opinion on what policies are best for the community are real and deep; as are differences of interest between different groups such as managements and workers, or more prosperous and less prosperous parts of the country, or the rich and poor worlds. But the hope would be that through a frank and searching examination of the issues we could arrive at a mutually acceptable minimum consensus as to what constitutes the public good in any situation. It should also lead to greater willingness to understand the aspirations and fears of other groups, and to modify one's own aspirations and fears enough to make a generally accepted policy workable.

Such a degree of agreement is difficult to achieve, but without it will it be possible, for instance, to introduce an effective remedy for inflation? This would have to involve some type of voluntarily accepted incomes policy, so that rising wage costs can be curbed without either intolerable unemployment, a continued decline in the exchange value of the currency, or draconian restrictions on imports.

(*c*) *Extension of the Welfare State principle beyond national boundaries*

We have already gone a considerable way towards accepting that the Welfare State principle of active concern for all groups in the community cannot be confined within the boundaries of national states. The crudely selfish concepts of 'national interest' characteristic of traditional diplomacy have been greatly modified by participation in such bodies as the International Monetary Fund, the General Agreement on Tariffs and Trade, the North Atlantic Treaty Organization and the European Economic Community. Already the latter has established a Regional Fund to provide assistance to poorer regions throughout the areas of the member states. It has also accepted a collective responsibility for aid to the Third World, of which the Lomé Agreement giving preference to former colonial territories in Africa and the Caribbean is a kind of first fruits.

In spite of the greater economic stresses of the 1970s, one would hope that this would be carried further. One would hope, for instance, that countries in difficulties with their balance of payments would abstain from unilateral imposition of import restrictions or exchange controls or devaluations, but would rather consult with their trading partners in order to arrive at methods by which they can help one another mutually.

This attitude is particularly necessary in the case of relationships between the developed and the developing worlds. Whatever the economic difficulties of the rich countries, and those of Britain in 1975 are real enough, they arise essentially out of a failure to manage our affairs properly. We still have the wealth and experience which give us an obligation to consider the needs of those caught up in the vicious circle of poverty. Our difficulties must not be made an excuse for being unwilling to give aid on terms which really help the recipients rather than burdening them, to open our markets to the manufactured goods which they can produce more cheaply than we can, to work out arrangements for the stabilization of primary product prices. No one concerned for justice between peoples can rest satisfied with the present imbalance.

This kind of wider concern for the welfare of those outside our own boundaries is again a field where Christians have a great responsibility. Only a faith which has a vision of all men as brothers because they are the children of one Father can provide the impetus towards such policies, which so often cut across the immediate interests of groups of people in our own country.

(*d*) *The world political preconditions*

If we are to work towards the fulfilment of such a vision of a welfare world, it can only be on the basis of a hard headed recognition of international political realities.

First, as we have seen in chapter 5, we have to accept that drastic political change, sometimes amounting to revolution, may be essential in many parts of the world before effective development can take place. The debacle of American intervention in South-East Asia has once again brought this home to us. In spite of all our uneasiness about revolutions and their effects, we must beware of the equal dangers of giving support to corrupt, inefficient and tyrannous regimes just for the sake of preserving stability.

Secondly, any vision depends upon the continuance of a balance of power between the superpowers, the United States, Russia and China. If this balance is not to break down, these powers must be willing to continue the process of *détente* between themselves and respect for one another's accepted spheres of influence. They must also be willing to localize and try to solve conflicts between lesser powers, such as those between Israel and the Arab States, between Greece and Turkey over Cyprus, or formerly between India and Pakistan.

This may seem a very unidealistic conclusion, and a long way from the universal reconciliation and disarmament which we should all like to see. But it is a recognition of the reality on which world peace has been based for thirty years now, and it in no way precludes efforts towards, for instance, an effective limitation of nuclear arms.

These suggested lines of policy may appear both limited and down to earth, a far cry from the vision of peace on earth and goodwill to men to which we are committed. Yet the essence of Christianity is that it is down to earth, based on one who came down to earth and accepted our life with all its frustrations and limitations. So we, too, while never losing sight of the fullness of the vision of a new heaven and a new earth which he made it possible for us to strive for, must be prepared likewise to earth our vision in immediate practical proposals.

NOTES

Chapter 2

1. This is not a work of Christian apologetics, concerned to explain and justify the basic doctrines of the faith to those unfamiliar with them. There are plenty of such works for those who need them. It takes the basic Christian position as given and seeks only to sum it up in words which will, it is hoped, find general acceptance.

2. Once again, we are not here concerned to discuss the significance of Christian experience in the light of modern psychological understanding of the human personality. We are merely summarizing this experience in the language in which it has been traditionally expressed.

3. The implications of this for traditional thinking about the working of the market economy, and the alleged beneficial effects of competition, in making self-seeking work for the common good, will occupy us in chapter 7.

4. Cf. Mark 10.23–27; Matt. 19.23–26; Luke 18.24–27.

Chapter 3

1. For an account of how the government can control the supply of money through its influence on credit creation by the banks, see any elementary textbook on money and banking, such as A. C. L. Day, *The Economics of Money*, 2nd ed., OUP 1968, or R. S. Sayers, *Modern Banking*, 7th ed., OUP 1967.

2. Cf. Irving Fisher, *The Purchasing Power of Money*, Macmillan, NY 1911.

3. *The Economist*, 13 September 1975, p. 75.

4. The following classification is based on that found in D. Jackson, H. A. Turner & F. Wilkinson, *Do Trade Unions Cause Inflation?*, section 2, CUP 1971.

5. The system of fixed exchange rate parities as agreed at the Bretton Woods Conference of 1944.

6. Cf. *The Economist*, 19 April 1975, p 80.

7. For a readable account of the Keynesian model of the economy see such books as M. Stewart, *Keynes and After*, 2nd ed., Penguin 1972, or P. Donaldson, *The Economics of the Real World*, Penguin 1973.

Chapter 4

1. F. Field, *Unequal Britain*, Hutchinson Arrow Books 1973, p. 24.

2. Ibid., pp. 26–7.

3. A. B. Atkinson, *Poverty in Britain and the Reform of Social Security*, CUP 1969, p. 38.

4. *Annual Abstract of Statistics 1974*, HMSO, tables 43 and 51.

5. Ibid., table 51.

6. Ibid., table 165.

7. *Social Trends 1974*, HMSO, table 132.

8. R. Davie, N. Butler & H. Goldstein, *From Birth to Seven* (National Child Development Study), Longmans 1972, p. 102.

9. *General Household Survey 1973*, HMSO, p. 233.

10. F. Field, op. cit., p. 58.

11. Cf. H. F. Lydall, *Journal of the Royal Statistical Society*, Part 1, 1959, table 7, p. 11 and F. W. Paish, *Lloyds Bank Review*, No. 43, Jan. 1957, table V, p. 11.

12. *Social Insurance and Allied Services*, Report by Sir William Beveridge, Cmd. 6404, HMSO 1942.

13. Cf. *Better Pensions*, Cmnd. 5713, HMSO, September 1974.

14. *Proposals for a Tax Credit System*, Cmnd. 5116, HMSO, October 1972.

Chapter 5

1. *Poverty Report 1974*, edited by Michael Young, Temple Smith 1974, table 11–1, p. 239 (from the article by Charles Elliott on 'The International Context of British Poverty').

2. *The Economist*, 1 March 1975, table on p. 76.

3. A. P. Thirlwall, 'The Development Gap', *National Westminster Bank Quarterly Review*, Feb. 1970, pp. 40–41.

4. *Partners in Development*, Report of the Commission on International Development (Pearson Report), Pall Mall Press 1969, p. 18.

5. Ibid., table 3–4, p. 74.

Chapter 6

1. For a detailed discussion of the concept of the gross national product see P. Donaldson, *Economics of the Real World*, Penguin 1973, ch. 3. The distinction between gross and net national products is that the latter excludes provision for depreciation, whereas the former includes it.

2. The crude birth and death rates measure the annual number of births or deaths per thousand of the total population. Their size is affected not only by the level of fertility and mortality, but also by age composition. Other things being equal, a population with a large proportion of old people in it will have a higher crude death rate than one with a lower proportion. Similarly, a population with a large proportion of young people will have a relatively higher crude birth rate than one with a lower proportion.

3. For instance, an American baby contrives by the time he grows up to consume annually over a million calories of food, 13 metric ions coal equivalent of energy (or 2,700 gallons of gasoline), 150 kg. of lead and of

copper, 100 kg. of aluminium and zinc, and 10 tons of steel. Cf. B. Ward and R. Dubos, *Only One Earth*, Penguin 1972.

4. *Partners in Development*, p. 33.

5. If all the land now cultivated were to be cultivated at the same level of efficiency as in the Netherlands, it has been estimated that the world could support 60,000 million people. (Lord Todd in *The Guardian*, 26 January 1972.

6. See R. Sinha, *Food and Poverty*, Croom & Helm 1975.

7. United Nations Statistical Yearbook, 1970, table 168.

8. Ibid., table 12. Energy consumption is expressed in tons of coal equivalent by converting the consumption of other kinds of primary energy such as oil or hydro or nuclear power into the tonnage of coal that would provide an equivalent amount of energy.

9. Denis Meadows, Donella Meadows, J. Randers & W. W. Behrens, *The Limits to Growth*, Earth Island Ltd 1972.

10. 'The Ecologist', *A Blueprint for Survival*, Penguin 1972.

11. W. Beckerman, *In Defence of Economic Growth*, Cape 1974, pp. 220–21.

12. On the problems of pollution see B. Ward and R. Dubos, *Only One Earth*, Penguin 1972.

13. W. Beckerman, op. cit., pp. 191–2.

14. Ibid., p. 193.

Chapter 7

1. For a fuller exposition of the basic working of an economic system, see G. Williams, *The Economics of Everyday Life*, 3rd ed., Penguin 1972, chs 1 and 2, or J. L. Hanson, *A Textbook of Economics*, 6th ed., Macdonald & Evans 1972, ch. 1, or any elementary economics textbook.

2. It is now accepted that many firms do not in fact seek to maximize profits, but have other aims such as maximizing the growth of sales, or perhaps a balancing of the aims of different groups within the firm. But this is possible mainly because competition does not force them to produce in the most efficient manner.

3. In practice competition is often more effective than this would imply, particularly through firms in other industries breaking into sheltered markets with new products.

4. Cf. A. B. Lerner, *The Economics of Control*, Macmillan, NY 1946, and O. Lange & F. M. Taylor, *On the Economic Theory of Socialism*, University of Minnesota Press, Minneapolis 1938.

5. Part ownership of firms by the government has been rare in Britain, though there are examples in British Petroleum and International Computers. In future it is likely to become more common, following the examples of British Leyland and Ferranti, in which shareholdings are being acquired in return for help in the supply of capital, and the plans to take holdings in North Sea oil firms.

6. *The Financial and Economic Obligations of the Nationalized Industries*, Cmnd. 1337, HMSO 1961, and *Nationalized Industries; A Review of Economic and Financial Objectives*, Cmnd 3437, HMSO 1967.

7. For instance, many economists maintained that if marginal cost pricing and target rates of return on new investments were prescribed, there was no need also to have overall annual target rates of earnings. On the other hand, it was argued that these gave an incentive towards efficiency and a standard to measure it by.

8. Parke *v.* Daily News, Ch. 927, 1962.

9. For a recent survey of producers' co-operatives, see 'The World of Co-operation', *The Economist*, 3 May 1975, p. 82.

Chapter 8

1. There is nothing new in this truth, of course. Earthly security can always be shaken by sickness, bereavement, financial loss, estrangement and the like. But the shaking of accepted patterns of life brings it home to us more clearly.

2. See chapter 7, pp. 159f.

FOR FURTHER READING

Wilfred Beckerman, *In Defence of Economic Growth*, Jonathan Cape 1974

Peter Donaldson, *Economics of the Real World*, Penguin Books 1973

—, *Worlds Apart*, Penguin Books 1971

R. L. Heilbronner, *An Inquiry into the Human Prospect*, Calder & Boyars 1975

D. Seers & L. Joy (eds), *Development in a Divided World*, Penguin Books 1971

John F. Sleeman, *The Welfare State*, Allen & Unwin 1972

John V. Taylor, *Enough is Enough*, SCM Press 1975

Barbara Ward & René Dubois, *Only One Earth*, Penguin Books 1972

Gertrude Williams, *The Economics of Everyday Life*, Penguin Books, 3rd ed. 1972

INDEX OF NAMES